THE HISTORY OF
Andrew Buchan's
RHYMNEY
BREWERY

by
Marion Evans

Foreword by
Roddy Llewellyn

This book is dedicated to my dear husband Roy
without whose help it could not have been completed.

Old Bakehouse Publications

Abertillery

First published in November 2007

ISBN 978-1-905967-07-0

Published in the U.K. by
Old Bakehouse Publications
Church Street,
Abertillery, Gwent NP13 1EA
Telephone: 01495 212600 Fax: 01495 216222
Email: theoldbakeprint@btconnect.com
Website: www.oldbakehouseprint.co.uk

Made and printed in the UK
by J.R. Davies (Printers) Ltd.

British Library Cataloguing in Publication Data: a catalogue
record for this book is available from the British Library.

Foreword

By Roddy Llewellyn

My association with Andrew Buchan's Rhymney Brewery took place almost fifty years ago, but my memories still remain vivid of my visits there with my father Lt. Col. Harry Llewellyn who was the Company Chairman from 1958 until its closure in 1978.

I am aware of the huge impact that the brewery made on the local community, from its conception by the Rhymney Iron Company in 1839 to its final demise as Whitbread Wales and I am sure that there is much that remains to be said about its changing history over the years.

Marion Evans has identified a need to fill this gap in Rhymney's social and industrial background and has produced this intriguing documentation on the brewery's past, laying particular emphasis, importantly, on the people who were employed there. She explores the Company's birth, its development over the years, the part that it played in World War Two, its wide sporting and social activities, its vast holdings in South Wales and much, much more.

The very mention of Rhymney and its brewery brings flooding back my recollections of the pleasant times that I spent there as a child during my father's visits. I distinctly remember playing in the yard there and the friendliness of the draymen as they prepared for their daily journeys. I remember spending many happy hours with the office staff and the warmth with which they greeted me. I especially looked forward to stealing a ride on the fork-lift truck with its very accommodating and happy driver. In all, good memories of a special time in my childhood.

I am really delighted to be asked to produce the foreword to Marion Evans' *'The History of Andrew Buchan's Rhymney Brewery'* which I am sure, will evoke many memories in the older generation of the community and provide newer generations with an insight into an important facet of the town's history.

I wish her every success with this publication.

Contents

Introduction

I have for many years harboured a desire to write a comprehensive history of the Rhymney Brewery. From 1839 to 1978, from the era of Andrew Buchan, the Brewery was to become an important focal point of activity in Rhymney and during its 140 years of production its development has been chronicled time and again. Each chronicle has, however, excluded what I consider to be the most important aspect of its history which is the people who worked there. The heartbeat of any organisation is its staff, in this case the coopers, draymen, managers, labourers, office workers and the many others who comprised this formidable workforce. A permanent record of the history of the Rhymney Brewery must in my opinion, not only include its early development, its growth, its changing phases and its deep involvement with the community, but also those individuals and personalities who made it all possible.

The Brewery, which was set up in 1839 by the Rhymney Iron Company was born, so it is recorded, from the need for the ironworkers to quench their huge thirsts following their shifts in the hot working conditions that they endured. A certain Scotsman named Andrew Buchan, its manager, was to become a historical figure in the town involved, as he was, with the controversial Truck Act, St. David's Church and the many other activities that were taking place. Buchan was a highly respected member of the community, much-liked for his kindness and benevolence towards the people. The Brewery steadily expanded, supplying beer to an increasing number of tied houses and by 1858 was reported as being the largest in South Wales. Further expansion continued over the years with the acquisition of a number of other breweries and by 1939 the Buchan estate numbered 362 hotels and inns. From dray-horses and steam-powered delivery wagons to early petrol lorries and pressurised tankers, the Brewery continued to ply its trade to all corners of South Wales and over the English border, from 1930 grandly displaying its famous Hobby Horse trademark.

The Company's demise in 1978 was a sad day for Rhymney and for the employees who worked there and by sharing my research of its past with the community through this book, I hope to produce a permanent record that will be of interest to today's and future readers. My list of acknowledgements gives a good indication of the level of interest that this publication has stimulated during the research stage. The fact that so many people within and outside the community, especially former Brewery employees, have willingly come forward with their memories and photographs has given me all the encouragement I need. To each of them I extend my warmest thanks.

I must particularly acknowledge the invaluable help given by Mr Nick Redman, the archivist at Whitbread plc when he visited Rhymney in 1992 during his own research into Whitbread in South Wales.

I am also extremely delighted to offer sincere thanks and appreciation to Roddy Llewellyn for taking the time and effort to write the foreword.

Finally I must thank my husband Roy for the extensive work that he has put into supporting me in the production of this book. As my reliable and level-headed *'ghost writer'*, he has given me every encouragement throughout and patiently organised my mass of research material in readiness for eventual publication.

Marion Evans

CHAPTER 1
The Beginnings

The Industrial Revolution in South Wales reached Rhymney in 1801 with the construction of an ironworks by the Union Iron Company in the Garn, near Llechryd, Rhymney Bridge. Rhymney House, which still exists, was the home of its manager and was situated, together with workers' accommodation, next to the ironworks.

The blast furnace, about thirty feet high, of the Union Iron Company built alongside a row of workers' cottages, later known as Granary Row, with the Manager's house in the trees beyond. In 1825 the Bute Ironworks came into existence and Rhymney's population began to explode from the influx of Welsh, Irish and English workers seeking their living in the new boom town.

Following the success of the Union Ironworks, further smelting development quickly ensued with the construction in 1825 of the Bute Ironworks.

Following earlier patterns established by neighbouring Dowlais, Merthyr Tydfil and Tredegar ironwork towns, it was not long before the Rhymney ironmasters' thoughts turned towards the profits that were to be gained by capitalising upon the thirsty needs of their workers when leaving the furnaces. Thus, in 1838, the Chairman of the Rhymney Iron Company, William Taylor Copeland, a Member of Parliament, Lord Mayor of London and later to become a porcelain manufacturer, recommended that a brewery be built *'for the supply of beer to all persons employed in the Works.'*

Up until then most workers had satisfied their thirsts by drinking barley water instead of spring water which tended to give them stomach cramp.

Copeland who lived from 1797 to 1868, was born an only son into an important Stoke Potteries firm. His father, William, was a partner to Josiah Spode and on his death, his son took over the Portugal Street branch, later in 1833, buying out the entire company in both Staffordshire and London with his partner Garrett.

During Copeland's engagement in the City of London he served as Sheriff and Alderman for the ward of Bishopsgate from 1828 to 1829 and as Lord Mayor of London in 1835 at the age of 38. Politically active, first as a Liberal and then as a Conservative, he died in 1868 at his home in Russell Farm, Waterford where he maintained a racehorse stud.

Their pottery marks are to be seen as Copeland & Garrett.

Copeland's recommendation for a brewery at Rhymney was quickly approved and a month later it was agreed that plans be drawn up by a Mr Kemp at a cost of 10 guineas. By January 1839 tenders were accepted for a Messrs. Pontifex to provide processing materials and other necessities at a cost of £2,225.

The headquarters of Messrs. Pontifex was in Shoe Lane, London and the Rhymney brewery maintained business links with them up until 1949. The above name-plate was built into the main walls of the brewery in recognition of this long-lasting association. The plate has been held at the Maritime Museum, Cardiff.

The construction of the brewery was soon under way and this was when a certain Andrew Buchan emerged as the one and only contender for its managership.

An early view facing west of Andrew Buchan's Brewery showing its position in relation to the surrounding area. At the top was Pidwellt Colliery, also known as The Barracks Level. On the extreme middle right is the Farmer's Arms which was originally a farm. Streets to be seen are Tre Edwards, White Row, Penuel Row and a part of Tre Evans. These days only Tre Edwards has survived.

This western view of the brewery was taken at a later date when St David's Church had been constructed, paid for by the Rhymney Iron Company.

CHAPTER 2

Andrew Buchan - A Profile

The new brewery took on its manager's name and here we see the entrance to the brewery yard with the familiar Andrew Buchan clock at its portal.

The name of Andrew Buchan is synonymous with brewing in Rhymney and for almost all of the Brewery's 140 years in existence it bore the name of its founder.

Buchan's first appearance in Rhymney was in the early 1820s where he worked as a carpenter in the Maerdy and Abertysswg Farms. He was born in Perth, Scotland but the Buchan clan originated from 1446 in an area called Achmakwy. The district of Buchan comprised the north-eastern part of Aberdeenshire and part of Banffshire and the title may have taken its name from 'bwch' which is Brython for 'cow', thus suggesting a cattle-farming background. It has been said that Andrew Buchan lived in Dumbarton before moving to Wales to make his living. Buchan's journey south to Rhymney, possibly by steamship to Milford Haven and from there by stagecoach, would have been long and arduous with frequent stops at local taverns during the coaching trek.

On his arrival in Rhymney he would have been faced with a contrasting panorama of sights and sounds.

Andrew Buchan (1787-1870) seen here aged 82, was a dominant personality in Rhymney throughout most of his lifetime.

This is a representation of the type of transport prevailing at the time, which Buchan may well have used for part of his long journey to the Welsh valleys.

The area was in a state of flux with the old farming communities being overtaken by a harsh industrial presence and a rapidly expanding population. His senses would have been struck by the noise, smoke and odour of the blast furnaces and he would have seen towering mounds of shale on the horizon. Ironworks were then situated close to the Rhymney River with their adjoining streams and feeder ponds to make optimum use of the water available and to drive their blast engines. Buchan would have observed however, that the upland areas, in many cases still forested, had maintained their original farmsteads. Oxen were still at work pulling ploughs; hay was scythed and sheep and cattle still summer-grazed on the surrounding hills. Most of the farmland on the Monmouthshire side of the Rhymney River had been bought up by Benjamin Hall who owned the Union Iron Company, having received it as a gift from his father-in-law Richard Crawshay. Thus Abertysswg and Maerdy Farms were both in the hands of the Rhymney Iron Company when Buchan started work there as a carpenter.

Dating back to the 16th Century, Abertysswg Farm, situated alongside the Nant Tysswg stream (Blaen Nant Tussocks), was one of the earlier farms in the locality and as such, experienced many of the considerable changes that have taken place in farming over the centuries. Its oak beams and panelled walls witnessed the clandestine meetings of priests and secret worshippers during the years of religious intolerance. Its fabric would have rung with the songs and recitations of young Welsh voices when the first attempts at schooling were practiced there. It would also have felt the affects of the cattle plague that swept through Wales in 1632.

Following his spell as a carpenter, Buchan, who was also a qualified mechanical engineer, was chosen in 1826 by the Rhymney Iron Company to divert the course and deepen the bed of the Rhymney River in order to expand the Bute Ironworks. This was a massive undertaking, requiring a huge force of navvies, working entirely with hand-tools to move thousands of tons of soil eastwards from the stretch of the river between the lower end of Rhymney to the Pontlottyn Bute area.

The dramatic transition from rural Rhymney to industrial Rhymney is beautifully depicted in this painting of the Rhymney Ironworks undertaken by Penry Williams at a time when Pontlottyn had yet to be built. It is reproduced here by kind permission of The National Library of Wales.

For such a project to be completed without the benefit of today's earth-moving equipment, brings home the enormous challenges that faced engineers in the early 1800s. The navvies (short for navigators) were a huge army of tough workmen who, sometimes working with local labour, moved around the country following railroads and canals that were continuously under construction. The South Wales navvies engaged by Buchan were often of Scottish, Irish and Welsh descent, armed with shovels, picks, barrows and importantly, packs of dynamite; they would be hired where and when their labour was required, either sleeping rough or in specially constructed huts.

Buchan's engineering and man-management skills would have been tested to the full during this construction project. Pay day for the navvies was the day when the locals would have stayed at home and locked their doors because of the drunken disruption, fighting and general lawlessness that prevailed until they returned to work, perhaps days later. Being subjected to such mayhem, local antagonism towards the navvies increased to such an extent that it was necessary for troops to be brought in to keep the peace. These troops were accommodated in huts along what is now Barracks Road, then called The Barrax. Further projects of straightening and embanking the higher reaches of the Rhymney River were also attributed to Andrew Buchan.

The Rhymney Iron Company had by now taken over Carno Shop which was previously a private concern owned by a Mr Edwards and in 1835, on the death of its first manager, Andrew Buchan was appointed his successor.

Carno shop as it looks today and inset, how it originally appeared. Also inset is a picture of its early manager Andrew Buchan as depicted on a drinking mug.

Carno Shop at Twyn Carno was a relic of the absolute domination that the Rhymney Iron Company's 'Company Shops' held over its workers, where anything from a matchstick to a shroud and coffin could be purchased and which once boasted its own candle-making workshop. It was here in 1835 that the astute Andrew Buchan introduced the Truck System, largely ignoring the 1831 Truck Act which had supposedly outlawed the system.

The new Lawn Company Shop, opposite the railway station, was opened by the Rhymney Iron Company in 1837 and Buchan, then aged 50, was chosen to manage it. He continued with the Truck System there, whereby goods supplied to employees were paid for by deductions from wages and in some respects, it proved beneficial to certain families who were subject to it. The ranks of the workers of the Company were often recruited from wandering labourers who would enter the shop in a destitute condition. No one knew them; no one could give them credit and they could not exist until their pay arrived.

Rhymney Iron Company workers at the Lawn Company Shop in 1900.

So, by arrangement with the Iron Company and the Shop, the stranger was supplied with food and the cost was deducted from his first pay packet. This was considered to be one excellent feature of the Shop that helped new workers, often penniless, to survive. Navvies, because of their special circumstances, were admirably suited to the fundamentals of the system and in fact, this was a reason by which Andrew Buchan got around their legal difficulties with the Truck Act. The downside was that workers became 'tied' to the Shop and controversy reigned supreme because of Buchan's persistence with what was widely publicised as a penuric method of trading. This, following his death, ultimately led to the 1886 *Rhymney Truck Case'* which once and for all ensured that *'There shall be no more Truck at Rhymney'.*

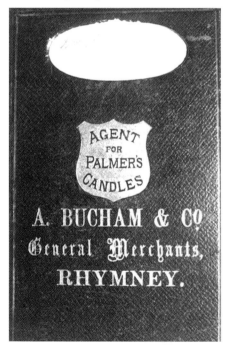

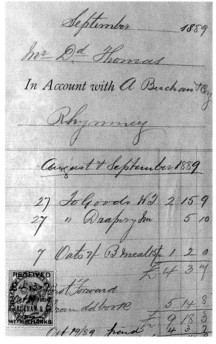

A Buchan account book and a bill signed and sealed with a Victorian penny stamp.

Under the system, being paid in goods meant that the workers had no cash and therefore had to pay in kind for any purchases that they themselves made. A bucket of coal for instance would have been a most useful piece of currency whilst a barber would take ale for giving a haircut as might a chimney sweep for cleaning the chimney. Candles and tobacco received from the Shop were bartered with or exchanged for money. Drinking was a problem and wives sometimes took their husbands' shoes and hats, wearing them to go shopping, thereby ensuring that their menfolk stayed at home with the children instead of scampering off to the nearest pub.

The Company Shops occupied a central and dominant place in the life of a smallish community like that of Rhymney. The Lawn Shop was a solid and stately building, standing in its own grounds, served by its own railway lines, with accommodation for grocery, drapery, ironmongery, furniture, butchery and baking departments, a slaughterhouse, stables, warehouse and offices. It did not possess the total monopoly of trade in the town however, as the High Street was interspersed throughout its length with small private shops and the workmen were free to make purchases there, providing of course that they had the money or were credit-worthy. In fact, in 1850, 437 workmen in the employ of the Rhymney Iron Company had no dealings with their Company Shop, 409 dealt partially whilst about 1,300 workmen were recorded as regular customers.

The fame of Andrew Buchan's Shop was widespread and he purchased goods from all the surrounding counties of Monmouthshire, Breconshire, Carmarthenshire and Cardiganshire. Weekly deliveries were received of fat cattle, pigs, sheep and poultry to be slaughtered on site. Eggs, cheese, butter, salted and fresh and flour were brought in by the ton.

Well-known were the Cardigan butter-men who were not averse to a spot of smuggling and who, together with their dairy products, would produce a few yards of Oriental silk or a keg or two of best brandy hidden away in their carts. Their arrival was often anticipated by far-seeing customers who would venture far out of their way to avoid other purchasers and the Excise men in their quest for the contraband goods.

The Lawn Truck shop closed in 1911 and this photograph shows it boarded up, and in a state of deterioration. As well as the Twyn Carno branch, other branches traded at Tirphil, Brithdir, Deri and Pontlottyn.

The name Andrew Buchan is today so firmly associated with the Rhymney Brewery that it is easy to forget how, in the 19th Century it was more for the Company Shops rather than the brewery for which he was better known.

This building was Buchan's family house when in charge of the Company Shops. It stood next to the Lawn Shop at the bottom of Surgery Hill and today houses Rhymney College. Its design is similar to houses in Bute Town with overhanging eaves and sturdy military-like structure, said to be influenced by Scottish architectural styles of the 17th to 19th Centuries and similar to patterns found in Lowther, Westmoreland.

The 1841 census indicated that the following people resided at Lawn House:-

Andrew Buchan, aged 52, shopkeeper, Scotland
Sybella Buchan, aged 46
Stuart Buchan, aged 21
Robert Hall, aged 22, Scotland
Gomer Stuart, aged 30
Elizabeth Jenkins, aged 30, servant
Margaret Miles, aged 26, servant
Jemima Edwards, aged 18, servant
Ann Edwards, aged 23, servant
May Edwards, aged 37, servant

This fascinating photograph is of four servant maids who were employed in Lawn House during the 1800s. It is not known whether they can be associated with the names mentioned above however.

This is the back end of Ty Mawr House that was to provide living accommodation, again with its servants, for chief executives of the Brewery. Among its tenants were Lt. Col. G.L.Hoare, CBE, one of its managers and Mr Pares, another. A young Mrs Beddoe, shown aside, was a servant at Ty Mawr before moving to Forge Street to live.

In 1839 Andrew Buchan took over the management of the Rhymney Iron Company's Rhymney Brewery which quickly expanded under his firm and astute guidance. An 1858 directory records that *'brewing is being carried on to a considerable extent by Andrew Buchan & Co. at Rhymney where the brewery is considered the largest in South Wales'.*

The Brewery took on its manager's name which remained with it for many years to come. Though a benevolent employer, Andrew Buchan was a temperance practitioner and a virtual dictator who banned the *'boozers'* from his workplace and ensured that they were fit for work. Ironically, he not only regulated the profits of his brewery but he also regulated the drinking habits of its labour force.

An early photograph of the Brewery from around 1900 with the coal trucks making their way from the Pidwellt drift mine. The Brewery shared the Rhymney Iron Company's rail line which extended into the Brewery yard.

Workers of the Rhymney Iron Company enjoy their 'daily pinta'.

Buchan continued to manage the Brewery until the 1850s during which time he endeared himself to the local community with his kindness and benevolence. His private life however, was not as happy as his public and business affairs. He had five brothers and sisters who all went to live and work in America, leaving him, his wife Sybella and son Stuart who was born in 1818 and who was to meet a sorry end.

Two commemorative jugs that were produced around the time of Andrew Buchan's death. He is seen here with his wife Sybella.

Son Stuart married a Margaret Williams of Merthyr Tydfil at St. David's Church, Rhymney in 1848 and they produced one child, Andrew Stuart, who sadly died of diphtheria in 1868 at the age of 14. They lived at Number 8, Buchan's Row, which is now The Terrace, Rhymney.

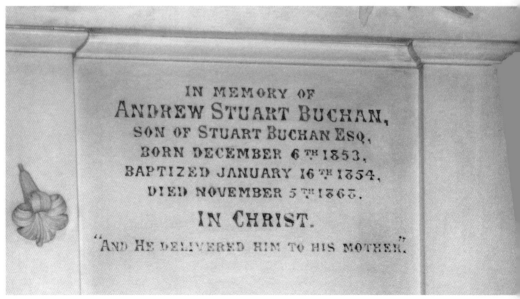

Wall plaques inside St. David's Church that commemorate the deaths of the young Andrew Stuart and his mother Margaret.

IN MEMORY OF

MARGARET BUCHAN,

THE BELOVED WIFE OF STUART BUCHAN, ESQ^R

OF THIS PLACE,

WHO DIED JANUARY 16TH 1858,

AGED 58 YEARS.

"THEM ALSO WHICH SLEEP IN JESUS WILL GOD BRING WITH HIM"

"COMFORT ONE ANOTHER WITH THESE WORDS"

Margaret had died ten years earlier in 1858 weakened by epilepsy and menorrhagia and this had a marked effect on Stuart's stability. When his father gradually phased out his own involvement in the running of the Brewery in 1850, Charles Lewis, a brewer there, took over the reins and is recorded as its manager in 1858. In 1862 Stuart is listed as manager of both the Brewery and the Company Shop and he undertook this role for a number of years. Difficulties arose however, when in 1869 he began to show signs of the mental disorder that affected him for the remainder of his life. He died insane in 1874 aged 56 years.

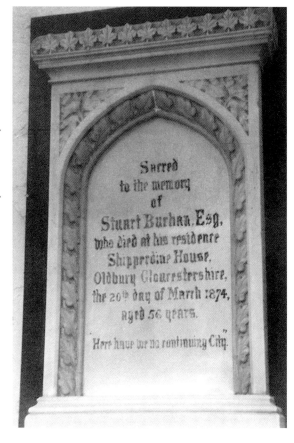

Stuart Buchan's wall plaque in St. David's Church.

Andrew Buchan and his wife were staunch members of St. David's Church, the construction of which was paid for by the Rhymney Iron Company. Royal Assent was given on 14th May 1839 to an Act of Parliament providing for *'An Act to enable the Rhymney Iron Company to erect and endow a church in the Parish of Bedwellty in the County of Monmouthshire'*. This led to the final construction and consecration of the church in 1843.

Rhymney Parish Church (St. David's) seen in grand isolation before the construction of its neighbouring houses had taken place. The bell-tower originally contained one bell which was presented to the church by Andrew Buchan, its first churchwarden.

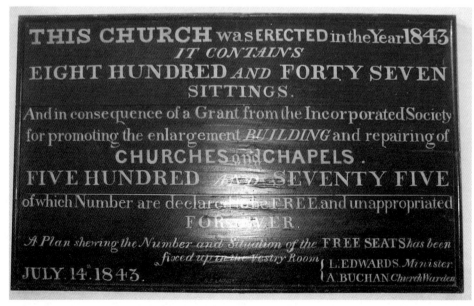

This plaque, placed in the church hallway, dated 14th July 1843, shows its attendance capacity and is endorsed by Lodwick Edwards, its first minister and by churchwarden Andrew Buchan.

Attended by his chaplain and chancellor, the visiting bishop was greeted at the church gate by clergy in canonical vestments, directors of the Rhymney Iron Company and by thousands of members of the public who had collected from neighbouring districts. Reverend Lodwick Edwards was appointed by the Iron Company and served as its first vicar from 1843 to 1855, when his health broke down through overwork and he died aged 55. Also in 1843, Alderman Copeland M.P. presented the church with its silver chalices. Following on from Lodwick Edwards came the much-admired Canon William Evans who served as vicar of the church from 1856 to 1900 and with whom Andrew Buchan went on to develop a strong friendship.

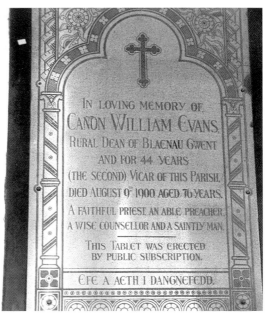

Canon Evans, here seen depicted on a jug, has a plaque on the church wall commemorating his 44 years as Parish vicar; he died aged 76. He was responsible, supported by the local community, for the introduction of the hugely popular 'Penny Readings' into Rhymney. This form of entertainment incorporated selected readings, singing and instrumental music and together with its demonstration of youth culture and self-expression, was to become increasingly competitive and in line with the small Eisteddfodau.

Buchan's bells were cast by John Warner and Sons, London in 1875 in Tenor B Flat. They consist of a complete ring of six, each inscribed with the maker's name and date of manufacture. One bell has the additional inscription *'In memoriam of Andrew Buchan who died on February 4th 1870'*. Buchan's bells have since become immortalised worldwide through the poetry of local poet Idris Davies and the global prominence that his lyrics of 'The Bells of Rhymney' has achieved through the efforts of such artistes as The Byrds, Jim Page, Judy Collins, Dick Gaughan, Cher, Robin Hitchcock, Bob Dylan, Pete Seeger and Mike Peters.

Throughout his life and particularly in his later years, Andrew Buchan earned great regard within the community for his kindness and generosity. Besides his business acumen, his human sympathies were always very much in evidence and many stories have been related of how he endeared himself to local people, especially the younger generation. One of his well-documented whims was, when he saw a small boy with a ragged cap, he would toss it over a hedge and then take the youngster to the store for a new one but the human touch is further revealed in the bag of biscuits that always accompanied the headwear.

On his death Buchan bequeathed in his Will the sum of £500 for the erection of five more bells to be added to the one already in the bell tower.

During a particularly lean period when food was short in the village, he magnanimously arranged for a shipload of iron to be sent to America in return for food which was distributed amongst the needy. Buchan also loved sport and would reward each member of the cricket team with a sovereign should they win their match. His attempts at trying to speak Welsh caused great amusement.

In his large home behind the Lawn Shop all were welcome. He had *'a pleasant parlour'* which was always warm and comfortable in winter with the smell of home-cooking emanating from the kitchen and bakery. Here traders doing business with him received a hearty welcome and were always paid on time.

His tact when dealing with his workmen was legendary and earned him great respect. On one occasion they broke into a wagon loaded with beer which was parked outside the Company Shop and consumed every vestige of the contents, a serious crime that would have called for a very serious penalty. Buchan however, in his diplomacy, met with the men the following day when they had sobered up and to avoid criminal proceedings, put it to them that they should accept a halfpenny deduction from their wages until the loss had been recovered. This they gratefully agreed to.

Buchan was also a prodigious snuff-taker, much to the distress of passing children into whose eyes the snuff sometimes blew; but the gift of a shilling invariably dried their tears.

This spill container depicts Andrew Buchan with the essential snuff box in his hands. Snuff-taking was so much a part of his character that most of his pottery shows him about to take a pinch.

The Brewery yard in the 1930s. Although many years after Buchan's death it retained his title until 1959.

The terms of Andrew Buchan's employment as manager of the Company Shop and Brewery included his entitlement to a quarter of the profits, guaranteed to be not less than £200 a year. He profited well and had made enough money by 1848 to purchase Shipperdine House, a grand mansion on the banks of the River Severn near Thornbury in Gloucestershire.

Shipperdine House, Thornbury as seen in 1860 with possibly Buchan standing on the balcony. It was here that his wife Sybella (who was born in Inverness, Scotland), died in 1856 and she is commemorated by the stained glass window in St. David's Church. The estate was gradually added to and when sold, in 1874, consisted of more than 140 acres.

A group of senior ladies of St. David's Church pose beneath the stained glass window which commemorates Andrew Buchan's wife Sybella. The group consists of Mary Irene Bartlett, Cissie Jones, Myfanwy Hughes, Nancy Jones, Barbara Rees, Agnes Owen, Eileen Davies, Mary Church, Thelma Barnes, Ursula Evans, Mary Hannah Roberts, Evelyn Harris and Eileen (Jones) Davies. Inset is church verger David Davies on the right and on the left is Cynthia Jones, now 95 years of age, the oldest church member and the oldest surviving ex-employee of the Brewery.

The Brewery prospered for thirty years with Buchan at the helm until his retirement in 1869. He died the following year at the age of 82 and was mourned throughout the valley.

Buchan's death was unexpected and followed a very short illness which developed while visiting a farm in Breconshire. His funeral was one of the largest ever seen in Rhymney. The Western Mail reporting his death said *'The Church Schools have lost a friend who was always ready to lend a helping hand. His liberality to the Church Cause on all occasions whenever help was required will endear his memory for all ages to come'.*

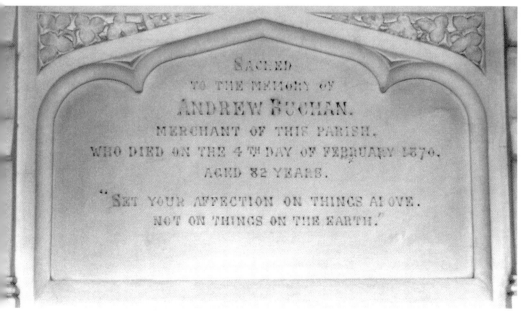

Andrew Buchan's commemorative plaque in St. David's Church. He and his family are entombed in the crypt of St. David's.

His Will included a bequeathal of £20 a year for 15 years *'for a treat to the teachers and scholars of the Rhymney Church of England, Day and Sunday Schools'*.

In view of the fact that his son Stuart was insane and his grandson had died, Buchan left his entire estate valued at £50,000 in the hands of trustees who, on the death of Stuart, were to distribute its proceeds equally among his brothers and sisters in America. With the deaths of Andrew and Stuart Buchan all connection between the Buchan family and Rhymney brewing came to an end except for the retention of the name over the years.

It is interesting to note that The Terrace, Rhymney, which housed the top officials of the Rhymney Iron Company was called Andrew Buchan Terrace when first built. At a later date however, its mainly Methodist tenants objected strongly to the association of their street name with a brewery and they successfully adopted the name The Terrace instead. In this photograph of The Terrace we see Mr Curtis, the great grandfather of Norman Gilbert and an employee of Andrew Buchan's in discussion with Doctor and Mrs Redwood.

CHAPTER 3
Post Andrew Buchan

Andrew Buchan officially retired in 1869, having given up the direct management of the Brewery in the 1850s. Brewer Charles Lewis took over in 1858, followed by Buchan's son Stuart in 1862 who continued until his mental disorder brought things to a halt. In 1871, possibly a little earlier, the Brewery and Shops' new manager was Richard Townley Johnson and he was followed by William Pritchard in 1874 who held the post for over 20 years. Pritchard was a native of Talybont-on-Usk who came in 1846 at the age of 14 years to work in the Lawn Shop having been brought up on a farm and country inn called Cross Oak. He made a favourable impression in his new post and was known for his liking for the Company horses and for matters agricultural. Tom Jones in his *'Rhymney Memories'* referred to him as *'an able and upright man of few words and rather forbidding exterior'*.

Under his direction the Brewery, still trading as Andrew Buchan & Co. continued to expand and by 1878 was delivering 12,500 barrels a year to its 29 tied houses in addition to its free houses. His success as a brewery manager however came to a sad and sudden end in 1898 when he shot himself with his revolver in the private railway sidings alongside the Brewery.

Following William Pritchard's death, his family donated the brass eagle lectern to St. David's Church in his memory which is pictured here with churchwarden Mr Evan Pugh. Pritchard was succeeded as Brewery manager by his nephew Francis Pritchard who left to take over the Western Valleys Brewery in Crumlin which he purchased in 1900.

TEL. Nº 2.

TELEGRAPHIC ADDRESS.
"BREWERY, CRUMLIN".

D. F. Pritchard, Ltd

BREWERS
AND
WINE & SPIRIT MERCHANTS.

Western Valleys Brewery,
Crumlin,
Mon.

THE TRUE BREW.

ALWAYS IN GOOD CONDITION.

CHAMPION GOLD MEDAL.

BREWERS EXHIBITION, LONDON.

This letterhead shows Francis Pritchard's Western Valleys Brewery, Crumlin and the many awards that it had won. More significantly however, it also shows the Hobby Horse logo 'The True Brew' that originated there and was later to be adopted by Andrew Buchan's Brewery when, in 1930, it took over the assets of the Western Valleys Company.

Some typical one-gallon stone jars bearing the Buchan markings which were used as fairly common containers many years ago and now regarded as collectors items.

CHAPTER 4

The Era of the Dray Horse

From the start, the Brewery delivered its product to local inns and taverns by horse and cart, some of which they rented from local farmers who might also lend their bigger horses for heavier dray work.

Older Brewery horses were often sold off to local businesses and this horse which pulled a water cart for the Rhymney Urban District Council is believed to be one such animal. Heavily bedecked with horse brasses it is attended by Mr Charles Bowen and his father Walter.

Before the Second World War, farmers would also take their horse and cart to the Brewery to collect spent grain from the mash tun which had been dried out and could be bought for 3d a bucket. Some spent grain could be fed to the Company horses but this had to cease during the war years when grain was commandeered by the government for conversion into cattle feed. By Pritchard's time the Brewery housed over 40 Clydesdale and Shire horses in its stables.

These magnificent animals, widely used in industry, stood over 17 hands high and were descended from 'The Great Horses of England', the medieval war horses. Strong but not speedy, their familiar feathered legs and white blaze enhanced their appearance when fitted out in full harness and brasses as they made their way pulling huge drays of barrels from inn to inn. The tradition of horse brasses goes back a long way to when the solitary farmer faced life overburdened with superstition and in need of charms and amulets to help him ward off evil spirits. Their deeply rooted primitive beliefs are carried forward today in decorative style with brasses of all descriptions being displayed on the showground or fair or wherever this splendid animal is on view. Some horses, some a ton in weight, needed a powerful hand and special care was taken by the Brewery to find handlers such as farmers and ploughmen who had sufficient strength and experience.

This fine Shire specimen was one of the Company's horses and is proudly displayed by ostler William Moseley outside the Maerdy stable in the 1930s.

This fine Shire belonged to Gwen Parfitt's father who hired it out to the Brewery from Old Furnace Farm in The Garn.

Recruitment for workers who were to handle the big horses was usually undertaken through such publications as the *'Hereford and Kidderminster Times'* which was why Welshmen, employed in the ironworks and unaccustomed to handling such animals, were never seen in this work. Farm workers jumped at the opportunity to take such work where they were paid the princely sum of 18/6d (about 93p) a week and a gallon of beer a day. This was a vast improvement on farming where they might have to work from dawn until dusk, bringing up a wife and four children on 9/- (45p) a week with a half-day holiday on Good Friday and Christmas Day each year. The Brewery also provided a house for 8/- (40p) a month, deducted from pay, to include a garden where crops could be grown for his family - a veritable fortune when compared to his previous existence.

Each drayman had three horses which he groomed daily and a four-wheeled dray that carried twelve barrels giving a gross weight load of 3 tons. Two horses were side-by-side in the shafts and the third, the leader, fixed in front.

Every horse owned by the Brewery was religiously recorded in their Horse Account, a copy of which can be seen overleaf for their March 1908-1909 record. Entries give the individual horse's identification, number, colour, name, age, the date it was purchased and from whom, its price, its last valuation, the date it was sold or disposed of, to whom and for how much. It would appear that by the age of ten, dray horses were 'worked out' and sold off to other concerns, with some around the year 1915, being requisitioned by the Army and taken away via Rhymney Railway Station. During their lives in the Brewery they were very well cared for and memories abound of the close relationship that built up between horse and draymen, who were known to cry at the loss of one of their friends.

Clifford Griffiths of Hill Street, Rhymney who worked for 51 years as transport engineer at Rhymney Brewery, treasured vivid collective memories of his and his father's experiences whilst working there. He has patiently chronicled the working life of his father Fred, a long-serving farrier with Andrew Buchan's Brewery whose job it was to help maintain the Horse Account during his employment there.

Fred Griffiths was born in St. Nicholas, outside Cardiff in 1858 or 1859 (the precise year is not known because the Registrar was drunk at the time!). His involvement with horses began at the large Cordrigton Estate where he became its Chief Stud Groom, caring for first-class hunters and coaching horses. He was articled to become a farrier and worked for the first year of five with no pay, the second year receiving 2/6d (12½p) a week, the third year 5/- (25p) and the fourth and fifth years 10/- (50p) a week. His indentures, written in copperplate on parchment, are presently on loan to Cardiff Museum.

Number.	Colour.	Name.	Age.	Date Bought	From whom bought.	Price bought at	Price last stock.	Date Sold.	To whom sold.	Price sold at.	Remarks.
			148	Brought Forward.			718 17 7				
21	Bay	Rattler	6	June 21 /07	Harvey Gloster	52	47 14				Exchanged in deal for Black Horse No 33 £6 allowed
22	"	Sergeant	7			60	54				Exchanged in deal for 2 Greys No 31 + 32 @ £60
23	"	Jack	9	Nov 21 /06	Rock House Hotel	37	33 6				
24	"	Bounce	6	" 20 /07	A. Thomas, Spedhimoor	48	43 4				
25	"	Tommy	6	" 18	Harvey Gloster	53	47 14				
26	"	Gloster	6	Jan 8 /08	"	50	45				
27	"	Topper (Nag)	6	" 29	"	48	43 4				
			194				1032 19 7				
			7.1		Average		36 5 2				
28	B.	Topper Prince	5	May 5 /08	D. Rees, Gelligaer	61					
29	. Mare	Lester	6		Flux Esq. Penmark	50					
30	"	Darling	5	May 10 /08	McMathie, thePont Lewisfon	47					
31		Major	14	June 10 /08	Rosd from Jamaica Riode	18		Sept 4 /08	Shot. incurable (Quittor)		
31	D. Grey	Nelson	5	July 15 /08	Harvey	55					
32	"	Bob	5	"	"	52					
33	Black	Darky	5	Feby 5 /09	Spencer Abergt	55					
34	. Bay	The Duke	9	Mar 22 /09	Edwards, Brickhowel	30					
		End of Mar /09			Average Age 7/4		Cost £34 15 7				

A typical 'Horse Account' for the period March 1908-1909 showing horses that had been purchased from other businesses in the area. Poor 'Major' was shot at the age of 14 because of an incurable ailment. 'Rattler' was sold off with a £6 allowance in order that 'Darky' could be bought and 'Sergeant' was exchanged for 'Nelson' and 'Bob'.

Fred Griffiths went on to set up his own business as a farrier called 'The Three Horse Shoes' at Birch Grove, Cardiff and close to Maindy Barracks, home of the Welsh Horse Regiment. Many of the Regiment's horses were taken to him for treatment together with the privately-owned mounts of the officers who were barracked there. There was a problem with the payment of their bills however and Griffiths often had to wait months for accounts to be settled and this caused difficulties within the business. This was when he came upon an advertisement for a farrier at Andrew Buchan's Brewery in Rhymney to tend to 42 dray horses with the assistance of three shoeing smiths. He thereupon applied and took the train up through the recently constructed Caerphilly railway tunnel for his interview

He turned out to be just the man they were looking for and was immediately engaged, remaining with the Brewery until his death in 1922 following a long illness. *'The company was very generous to him indeed and he received his full pay for five years to the day he passed away'* says his son Clifford.

As a farrier Griffiths' responsibility was to ensure the well-being of the Company horses. Each horse had its own straw-bedded stall with its name painted brightly above and each knew exactly which stall was theirs. They were fed the best hay, cut into chaff and mixed with dried beans, peas, nuts and oats. Griffiths recalls such names as Boxer, Duke, Tiger, Beauty, Lion, Sandy, Mighty and Stingo. He also remembers the five or so cats that lived in the stables, each of which had its favourite horse on which to sleep, much to the apparent pleasure of its bed-mate.

The dray-horse's working day was from 6am to 6pm during the week and from 6am to 2pm on Saturdays. Each had a wool-lined waterproof sheet in the dray to protect against the rain and heaven help the drayman should any return with a wet back. Their intelligence and homing instinct became legendary and on many a dark winter's night, they could be seen bringing home a sleeping drayman through darkened streets from faraway neighbouring valley towns. The leader always seemed to know its way home and would occasionally stop, instinctively, for the team to rest for a few minutes before moving on.

Injured or ailing horses would be sent to the Company's farm below Pontlottyn or to the old vicarage field at Nantllesg to aid their recovery. As a farrier one of Griffiths' jobs was to give medical attention to the dray-horses. He remembers amputating the leg of a small horse and replacing it with a wooden one after which the horse became capable of undertaking light duties. He also had the unpleasant task of putting down severely injured horses, which invariably brought considerable grief to their associated draymen.

For his long and valued service with the Brewery, Fred Griffiths was awarded the silver medal pictured here. The goldsmiths and silversmiths who were commissioned to produce the medals by the Brewers and Allied Traders were WF Ranger and Sulley of London. First awarded in 1908 under the Chairmanship of T Edwards, they continued to be presented until the 1920s when they were replaced by a gold shield.

Anciently linked with farriers, blacksmiths and the local Waun Fair at Pantywaun was the secret society of Horse Whisperers. This society was strongly represented throughout the country during the time of horse-power and was mainly kept alive through farmers and gypsies. A Horse Whisperer was basically a horse trainer who adopted a sympathetic view of the motives, needs and desires of the horse, based on equine psychology. The term goes back to the early nineteenth century when vicious and intractable horses that had suffered abuse and trauma were rehabilitated by secret methods. They were a powerful society until the advent of motorised transport but they still exist to this day and their skills are still held in high regard.

Horse Whisperers organised themselves into Masonic-type guilds with secret handshakes, passwords and salutes and were very much sought after. They did not, in fact, have magical powers as thought but used a close bond or identity with the horse they were treating, building a relationship with it 'in their own language'. They were skilful handlers, possessing 'horse sense' and a shrewd knowledge of horse psychology. They supported their treatment with techniques based on the horse's sense of smell. Obnoxious substances placed in front of the horse or on the animal itself would make it refuse to move. This was known as 'jading' the horse and they were happy to encourage the belief in a supernatural element to their work in order to protect their knowledge. Their ability to make a horse stand still as if bewitched earned them the name of 'horse witches'. Their 'jading' substances were many and varied and included stoats and rabbits liver, dried and powdered up with 'dragon's blood' (their code name for a red-gum resin extracted from a sort of palm-fruit). Aromatic oils were widely used such as origanum, rosemary, cinnamon and fennel together with attractive tit-bits such as sweet-scented cakes and gingerbread. A talisman that they all possessed was a frog's or toad's bone which they obtained through a complicated ritual of drying the dead frog or toad on a whitethorn bush for 24 hours, then burying it in an ant-hill for a month. The skeleton would then be tossed into a stream at full moon until a little crotch-bone separated itself and floated to the surface. This is the bone that was kept and which could 'jade' or 'un-jade' a horse by touching it on different parts of the body.

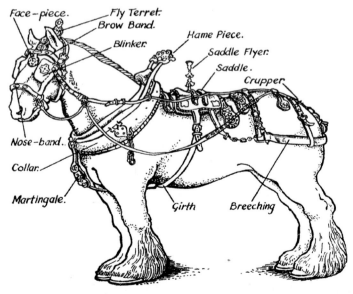

A Shire horse and its harness.

CHAPTER 5
Early Brewing

Many licensed houses in earlier days had their own brewhouse from which they obtained their own supply of ale for selling. The Blast Furnace Inn at Pontlottyn was such an example equipped, as it was, with an attached 14-barrel plant.

The Blast Furnace Inn in 1914 which at the time had M Cook as its proprietor and during which year it was bought by Andrew Buchan's Brewery. The inn was originally a farmhouse called Ty Gwyn, owned by Jenkin Edwards in 1825 and later converted by him in order that Pontlottyn ironworkers could quench their thirsts there. He aptly named his inn The Blast Furnace because of his employment as a manager in one of Rhymney's blast furnaces. It is said that he died in 1850 and his tombstone can be seen near the entrance to Gelligaer Church.

Farms, as well as inns and taverns practiced making their own ale and their establishments were often called malthouses. Traditionally, beer that was made with hops was called beer and that which was made with malt was referred to as ale, but these distinctions no longer apply. Malting is one of Britain's oldest industries and malt is the main ingredient in beer, providing the alcohol, most of the flavour and virtually all of the colour of the beer. It can be made from most grain, including barley, rice, oats and wheat. Malting is the controlled germination of cereals (normally barley). The grains are soaked in warm water for about a week to allow germination, which is known as 'chitting'.

The sprouted grain is then heated in a kiln to terminate the natural germination and then heated further to produce the required colour and biscuit flavour - the higher the temperature, the darker the colour and richer the flavour. The quality of the beer depends so much on the water supply and Andrew Buchan's mountain water was renowned for its purity.

Tommy Edwards unpacks a sack of malted barley which has arrived from Wakefield in readiness for loading into the mill where it will be crushed into a coarse flour.

"Here's a Health unto His Majesty."

All Loyal Subjects will drink this toast in a bumper of

BUCHAN'S (RHYMNEY)

KING'S ALE,

A pure Ale brewed only from the finest
English MALT AND HOPS.

Analyst's Report.

The Laboratory, Dock Street, Newport, Mon.
March 11th, 1902.

Messrs. A. Buchan & Co.,

Dear Sirs,

I hereby certify that I have analysed a sample of your "Buchan's Rhymney King's Ale," and beg to report to you as under:—

It is a very delicate Pale Ale of sound constitution and good body, possessing a clear bright colour, and of excellent aroma. The results of my analysis are such that I am in a position to speak most highly of its purity and general wholesomeness; and I am of opinion that it is a pure product of Malt and Hops.

It is free from acidity, and being clean and containing a good proportion of alcohol, its keeping properties are undoubtedly good. In flavour, appearance, and general quality it will, in my opinion, bear favourable comparison with all first-class Pale Ales.

I am, dear Sirs,

Yours faithfully,

(Signed),   GEORGE R. THOMPSON,

COUNTY ANALYST.

This County Analyst's letter to Messrs. A. Buchan & Co. gives firm evidence of the high quality of the Brewery's popular Kings Ale. Kings Ale was introduced in the Brewery in 1902 to mark the coronation of King Edward VII. The spring water used in its production was collected in two water tanks above Nantllesg House, known as Nantllesg Fach and Nantllesg Fawr. The water originated from an old ironstone pit nearby, Nantllesg Pit, which was 252 feet deep. It was this cool, fresh water pumped into the Brewery that gave the beer its distinctive taste. Other ales included Empire, GHB, BB, IPA and Stingo in draught and light ale, Empire Special, Cream Stout and Family Stout in bottles.

Self-brew farmers and innkeepers, to make stronger beer, perhaps for Christmas, used eight or nine gallons of spring water for every bushel of malt. For weaker beer, to be used at the hay or corn harvests, the amount of water used would be increased to fourteen or fifteen gallons. The equipment they used was basic with gorse or wheat straw utilised to plug draining vessels and old blankets to cover and warm the seedlings. Hops, brown sugar and yeast would be added to produce the final product.

Industrial brewing was, of course, far more sophisticated, mechanised and chemically more finely balanced. Buchan's employed only highly qualified technical and practical staff; their water supply had proved uniquely suitable over a number of years. They purchased the higher grade malts and hops at the correct seasonal time and their storage arrangements were properly regulated.

The malt storage rooms were situated on the highest floor of the brewery malthouse and delivered sacks of malt had to be hoisted skywards to be stacked. This was when the Company horse was brought in to lift the sacks from the yard floor by rope through the pulley blocks fixed to the top storey. This became such a routine chore to the horse that it would eventually go through its paces without any leading, walk up the yard in order to hoist a sack, wait for it to be unloaded and then return unbidden to the foot of the hoist to await the next load. In later years this horsepower was replaced by a steam engine invented by a blacksmith from Rhymney Bridge and then finally an electric motor superseded all.

The successor to Francis Pritchard as Brewery Manager was Captain T Edwards

who was responsible for their first acquisition when he bought the Crown Brewery at Pontypool in 1902. The Crown's estate of 14 licensed houses was some distance from Rhymney, spreading from Newport through Cwmbran at Abersychan and Garndiffaith with another five houses further away in Usk. This extended territory made it difficult for horses to make daily deliveries, so a steam lorry was purchased in 1908, followed soon afterwards by two more. Most of the finest redundant horses were later shipped to France for the War Effort and never seen again.

The large tower in the Brewery yard which housed the malthouse in its upper level.

CHAPTER 6
Early Transport

Andrew Buchan's first steam-powered wagon achieved the hair-raising speed of 8mph and proved a major success in the Company's development into a wider territory. The new steam locomotive was manufactured by Clayton & Shuttleworth and on the left stands Teddy Williams, father of Vivienne Williams who lived in Tre-Edwards. The person next to him is unknown but the driver is George Appleby. On the right is Bill Sims.

Despite their slow speeds, steam wagons still had their dangers and it was not long before the first casualty was to be reported when a seven-year-old lad was run over and killed on Rhymney's High Street.

This is the handwritten report relating to the aforementioned tragedy.

Here, proudly displayed in 1914, we have the first petrol-driven lorry to be used in Rhymney belonging to the Andrew Buchan Brewery. We are told that some of the characters shown are Clive Griffiths cranking the engine with his father Fred Griffiths leaning on the mudguard. Sid Allen is standing on one leg next to Tom Williams the father of Joe 'Bacus' Williams whilst on the extreme right is said to be John Rowley.

Pictured in 1935 is Mr Sid Allen, a long-serving driver for the Company with his 'No.5' petrol lorry outside the yard entrance. The photograph was taken by Mr GL Pares, Brewery Manager at the time.

The Brewery yard in the days when a railway engine made deliveries and petrol lorries were in use.

Seen here is an excursion from Rhymney Brewery in the late 1920s in a charabanc called 'The White Hope'. This was typical of the developing means of transport following the 1914-18 war years. Many ex-servicemen bought former War Department vehicles from their gratuities and used them for haulage work. Others innovatively converted their lorries into open coaches, fitted seats which gave birth to the lorry-bus or charabanc with its solid tyres and canvas hood. These vehicles were to open up the countryside and seaside resorts to all and sundry with trips to Barry Island, Gilwern Canal and other popular spots becoming a distinct reality rather than a mere dream. The 'White Hope' was an ex-WD lorry that had undergone such a conversion, on this occasion by Charles Hill, who went on to build his very successful transport business 'Hill's Coaches'. Seats were in rows of six and three passengers would sit beside the driver.

Another of the Brewery's petrol lorries, a Thorneycroft 1919 which was bought second-hand from the Government after the First World War. Parked in the Brewery yard with the Andrew Buchan clock conspicuously in sight, two of the attendants can be identified as Sid Hughes and Harry Mobley.

Another charabanc prepares to leave the Brewery yard for an outing. With its silver bonnet, black hood, solid tyres and flags flying it would have undoubtedly attracted much attention on its journey.

Some of the fleet of trucks belonging to the Brewery parked military style in the outside yard. The yard, which was cobbled to allow the dray horses a good foot-hold has been preserved today as a relic of the Brewery and can still be seen alongside the car park at Aldi's supermarket.

This 'Buick' car pictured in 1919 was purchased by the Company for use by their travelling salesman Mr Dickens who is seen here prepared to set off on his rounds. The car had four solid rubber tyres but not equipped with a spare wheel.

A later-designed dray parked at the bottom of Goshen Street with its driver Reg
Edwards accompanied by a relative paying a visit from Australia during the 1960s.
The 'Hobby Horse' synonymous with the Rhymney Brewery is proudly displayed on
the roof of the cab.

The ultimate delivery vehicle was the pressurised tanker, seen here in the outside
yard. The 'Hobby Horse' prominently placed on the roof was replicated from a three-
dimensional model fashioned by Graham Gilbert for an earlier carnival.

Further Developments

GL Pares, who is said to have sailed his yacht on Newtown Pond, succeeded Captain Edwards as Brewery manager in 1915 and continued in that role until his retirement in 1935; but many difficulties had to be overcome during his time in office. Following the War Years and the national miners' strike in 1921, an *'extreme depression'* descended on the Brewery, as it did with other breweries throughout South Wales and there was a great danger of Rhymney being sold off or closed. By this time, after the closure of the Company Shop in 1911, Andrew Buchan & Co. had become, for the first time, solely a brewing business within the Rhymney Iron Company. By April 1920 however, the Powell Duffryn Steam Coal Company Ltd. Acquired the RIC and took over the collieries and the Brewery. Powell Duffryn's decision to dispose of the Brewery because of the difficulties they were experiencing, involved prolonged negotiations with other companies. Efforts to sell out to Hancock's of Cardiff in 1923 proved to be abortive. Amalgamation talks with Wintles Brewery of Mitcheldean and Webbs of Aberbeeg came to nothing and by 1928 the situation had become most serious. It was decided that strict economies should be made in every department of the Brewery, including salary reductions of officials and staff which helped ease the situation to some extent. It was evident however that an amalgamation with one of the larger brewery interests was not possible and that arrangements with smaller privately-owned breweries should be explored. Success was achieved, when in 1929 Buchan's Brewery and Griffiths Bros. of Blaina joined to form a new company which was called Andrew Buchan's Brewery Ltd. with its first chairman being Lt Col GL Hoare, CBE who went on to hold the post for 23 years. The Brewery had at last become a Company within its own right and a new era in its history was about to begin. Steady expansion ensued and in 1930, most of the assets of DF Pritchard Ltd. of the Western Valleys Brewery in Crumlin were obtained - the very same Pritchard who had left Andrew Buchan & Co. in 1900.

The first chairman of the new Andrew Buchan's Breweries Ltd. Lt Col GL Hoare.

PRITCHARD'S CRUMLIN
AUTUMN ALE

THE ALE THAT STAYS WITH YOU
AND KEEPS THE COLD OUT

The Pritchard family crest, shown on the adjacent bottle, bears the representation of a horse which was later adapted by them to a huntsman and used for advertising, such as upon the above playing card. The 'Hobby Horse' was adopted, it is believed, from this concept.

The DF Pritchard Ltd. Brewery was situated on Viaduct Road below the famous Crumlin Viaduct which had been constructed in 1857 and demolished in 1965. It carried the Neath to Pontypool railway line across the Ebbw Valley. Pritchards had holdings in Ystrad Mynach, Ebbw Vale, Bedwas and as far north as Troedyrhiw and Merthyr Tydfil.

The Taff Vale Brewery dated back to the 1840s and was one of the holdings of DF Pritchard Ltd. taken over by Andrew Buchan's Breweries Ltd. in 1936. Widely known as 'The Taff' it was the last producing-brewery in Merthyr Tydfil. It was situated close to the old canal and River Taff, which enabled barges laden with malt or hops to come right up to the wharf from Cardiff.

At the time that the Taff Vale Brewery was taken over by Buchan's in 1936, Buchan's had an estate of 25 freehold and leasehold houses. By 1939, the Buchan estate numbered 362 hotels and inns, most of which were in Monmouthshire and Glamorganshire.

The Taff Vale Brewery was founded by Thomas Evans and was in the Georgetown area of Merthyr. In 1904 the brewery moved to completely new premises on the hill above Penydarren Road in 'a large block of imposing and well-equipped buildings which were designed by Llewellins and James of Bristol.

By obtaining the Pritchard estate Buchan's also inherited the now famous trademark of its 'Hobby Horse'. Synonymous with the Rhymney Brewery is the 'Hobby Horse' which remained a formidable symbol of the Company from soon after Col. Hoare's appointment until the time of the Brewery's closure. The 'man on the barrel' was designed by a keen sportsman, one of the Pritchard's brewing family in Crumlin.

Further expansion continued and D Williams & Co. (Merthyr) Ltd. was taken over by Andrew Buchan's Breweries in 1936. Col. AJD Griffiths was Chairman and Managing Director of D Williams at the time and he joined the Andrew Buchan Board as General Manager. In 1952 he replaced Lt Col. Hoare as Chairman on Hoare's retirement until he himself retired in 1958.

Col. AJD Griffiths became Chairman of Buchan's in 1952. He was Deputy Lieutenant and High Sheriff of the County of Monmouthshire and a Justice of the Peace. He had also been Master of the Tredegar Hunt for some years and was an active member of the Brewers Society. He was also Chairman of the South Wales Brewers Association and of the Herefordshire, Monmouthshire and South Wales Branch of the National Trade Defence Association.

Also acquired in 1936 was the controlling interest in Crosswells Brewery Ltd. thereby extending Rhymney's estate into the Caerphilly and Cardiff areas.

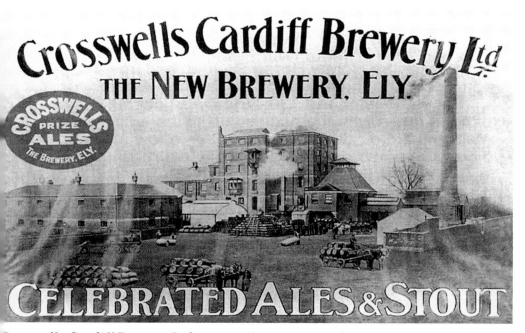

Crosswells Cardiff Brewery Ltd. originally incorporated in 1892, was established to sell beers in South Wales for Walter Showell & Sons Ltd. of Oldbury, Worcestershire as well as Bass and Guinness. At the time of its acquisition by Buchan's it was described as 'one of the largest brewing enterprises in Wales'.

Andrew Buchan's Breweries Ltd. was by now quite a sizeable concern; trading was looking up and further expansion was imminent. Their next acquisition was to be the Reform Brewery Co. Ltd. of Abersychan which they took over in 1939. This small brewery, founded in 1832, had acquired Westlake's Brewery Ltd. near Blaenavon and this represented the largest part of the estate taken over by Buchans.

Charles Francis Westlake commenced brewing in Blaenavon in 1885 and his Westlake's Brewery Ltd., by 1907 owned 18 public houses. In 1904, having suffered from serious water shortages in Blaenavon, they built a new brewery a mile or two down the valley at Cwmavon. The new brewery situated on the east bank of the Afon Llwyd was a five-storey building designed by George Adlam & Sons of Bristol who were leading architects of the time and was one of the few to have survived demolition. Business declined during the 1920s and brewing finally came to a halt in 1928. It then merged with Daniel Seys Davies' Reform Brewery which had been founded in the same year as the Reform Act, 1832, eventually in 1939 to be taken over by Andrew Buchan's Breweries Ltd.

As far back as 1927, Buchans were preparing negotiations for the merging of the interests of themselves with Webbs (Aberbeeg) Ltd. but proceedings were held up when it emerged that the Scottish Finance Co. Ltd. were about to submit a fairly substantial cash offer for purchase of the undertaking of Andrew Buchan & Co. The offer did not materialise however and negotiations resumed with Webbs. Agreement could not be reached on amalgamation arrangements and valuation, however and the Webbs Board resolved that they were unable to entertain the proposals.

During the Second World War, Buchans continued to purchase more 'free houses' and most of the properties of the Herefordshire and Tredegar Brewery were taken over during this time. Leasehold properties were also obtained and by 1945, almost 90% of the Company's holdings were free-hold. At the end of the war in 1945, the entire share capital of Charles Edwards' Llanfoist Brewery, Abergavenny was purchased, together with a large share-holding of Crosswells Brewery in Cardiff. In November of 1951 Col. Whitbread and JE Martineau joined

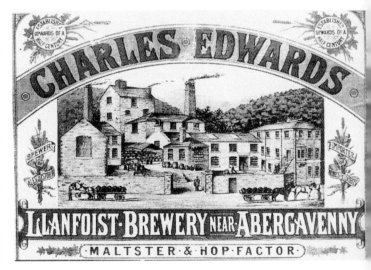

the Board of Andrew Buchan's Breweries Ltd. thereby associating Whitbread & Co. with the Rhymney concern and soon Whitbread's bottled beers and Mackeson Stout, which was now being bottled in Rhymney, were being sold throughout Buchan houses. In 1952 many more pubs bore the heading of 'Rhymney & Crosswells' and this was to gradually spread through the estate.

Lt. Col. Harry Llewellyn succeeded Col. Griffiths as Chairman of Andrew Buchan's Breweries Ltd. in July 1958.

Lt. Col. Llewellyn CBE was Chairman at Rhymney for many years and will be particularly remembered for his sporting achievement when winning a gold medal for Great Britain in the equestrian event of the 1952 Olympic Games in Helsinki on his famous jumper 'Foxhunter'. He was the senior National Hunt steward at Chepstow racecourse where, in 1959, was held the first Rhymney Breweries Steeple-chase to which the Company contributed 1,500 sovereigns as prize money - the most valuable prize ever offered for steeplechasing in Wales or the Border Counties. In this photograph Lt.Col. Llewellyn is seen presenting a silver jewel case to Hilda Price in 1968 on the occasion of her twenty years service with the Company. Hilda retired in 1978 following thirty years with the Brewery.

In March 1959 Llewellyn proposed that the name of the Company be changed to Rhymney Breweries Ltd. He felt that the name of Andrew Buchan had by now served its purpose but that it should now be updated to ensure that their product could be associated with Rhymney.

The new title was accepted and adopted in May 1959. That same summer the Brewery signed a 25-year Trading Agreement with Whitbread & Co. In 1959 the then Rhymney Breweries Ltd. also had the opportunity to acquire the Ely Brewery Company of Cardiff and by January 1960, had bought 90% of its outstanding equity. This was a major merger, with Rhymney having 470 pubs and hotels and Ely 260.

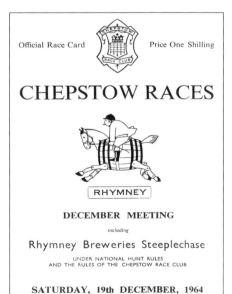

Official Race Card   Price One Shilling

CHEPSTOW RACES

RHYMNEY

DECEMBER MEETING

including

Rhymney Breweries Steeplechase

UNDER NATIONAL HUNT RULES
AND THE RULES OF THE CHEPSTOW RACE CLUB

SATURDAY, 19th DECEMBER, 1964

PROOF—17.3.59.

ANDREW BUCHAN'S BREWERIES, LIMITED

BREWERIES OFFICES,
RHYMNEY,
MON.

March, 1959.

DEAR SIR OR MADAM,

Your Company was incorporated in 1929 with its present name and before that date traded under the name of Andrew Buchan & Company.

For over 50 years most of our products have been known as " Rhymney " or " Rhymney Beers", I therefore feel that this link with the past has served its purpose and that we should bring the name of the Company up to date to ensure that our beers, wherever sold or displayed, can be associated with Rhymney, by which name they are advertised and popularly known.

It is therefore suggested that the name of the Company is changed from :—
ANDREW BUCHAN'S BREWERIES, LIMITED,
to
RHYMNEY BREWERIES, LIMITED.

Notice of an Extraordinary General Meeting to be held on
for the purpose of passing a Special Resolution to effect this alteration, together with Form of Proxy, is enclosed.

Yours faithfully,

H. M. LLEWELLYN,
Chairman.

B., M. & Co., LTD. T110910L.

Lt. Col. Llewellyn's letter to the Company proposing that a change of title had now become appropriate.

Ely Brewery was founded in 1850, being called the Tower Brewery in 1875 and in 1887 was registered as the Ely Brewery Co. Ltd.

One of the Ely Brewery's delivery drays as seen in about 1930.

Rhymney had, for many years, wanted to get their hands on the Ely holding rather than see it fall into 'competitive hands'. Ely had, over the years, made considerable investment and mergers with a number of Rhondda Valley breweries and had gained a reputation as one of the largest and most progressive companies in Wales and the West of England. The Chairman at Rhymney, Lt. Col. Llewellyn, would have preferred to have kept the Ely Brewery going as a complete concern but it became clear that their two breweries in Cardiff - Ely and Crosswells, just a few hundred yards apart, would require some sort of integration. One option was to concentrate all brewing in Crosswells and to use the Ely site for offices, which could also house the majority of clerical staff from Rhymney. Crosswells alone however, would be unable to meet the increased demand so it was decided to considerably extend their premises and to shut down the Ely Brewery. The new offices and a canteen were built nearby and together with the new brewery, were officially opened in March 1963. The re-modelled brewery had an output of 21,600 half-pints of bottled beer and 200,000 pints of draught beer a week.

Rhymney Breweries had by now, over 700 licensed houses ranging from Leominster in the east, Cardiganshire in the north and Pembrokeshire in the west. During this time however, in the early 1960s, the Brewery was faced with the dilemma of a declining coal industry and rising unemployment which was having a marked effect on their sales. Miners had to tighten their belts and make do with less beer money. The less-profitable public houses, caused by this economic change had to be closed and new pubs opened in more favourable areas such as developing housing estates, together with hotels in places such as coastal areas where industrial growth was taking place. It was in 1963 that the completely new Foxhunter Inn was opened in Hereford, the first in the city to be owned by the

Brewery. Named after Harry Llewellyn's famous mount, the pub had a specially constructed display case showing the major international awards that they had won between 1948 and 1953, including the Helsinki Olympic Gold Medal.

Financial pressures continued to grow at Rhymney through keen competition from other breweries and in 1965, Whitbread made their bid for Rhymney Breweries Ltd. This resulted in 1969 in a new company, Whitbread Wales Ltd. being formed from the merger of Evan Evans Ltd. of Neath (taken over by Whitbread in 1967) and Rhymney Breweries Ltd. The Chairman was Lt. Col. Llewellyn and the brewery remained in the hands of Whitbread Wales Ltd. until its closure in 1978.

This is a rear view of Whitbread Wales Ltd. Brewery, Rhymney before its closure in 1978.

The Workforce

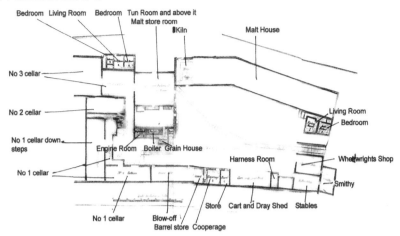

The above plan shows the layout of the Andrew Buchan's Brewery in the early 1900s when it still had its rail link with the Lawn Company Shop, which closed in 1911. Another outside linked rail line continued on to Pidwellt Pit, or the Barracks Level, which was situated opposite the brewery on the other side of the Rhymney River. Incoming goods such as hops, grain and malt were delivered to the Mill House for unloading on the brewery railway line. The Brewery's stables and smithy, with wheelwrights and dray shed were situated to the left of the entrance while the processing plants and malthouse were opposite, on the other side of the yard. It can be seen that living accommodation was provided for managers and brewers.

Some administrative staff who were engaged at Rhymney in the early part of the twentieth century were, from the back row, left to right: Unknown, Fred Istance who worked in the General Office, Will Bassett of the Yard Office, Beatty Evans, Albert Evans, Ron Cox who was employed in the General Office, Tom Jones and an unknown. In the front are William Cox from the General Office, David Bevan the Yard Office, GL Pares, MA General Manager, unknown and finally WJ Jones.

WJ 'Bill' Jones, also known as 'WJ' later moved on to Webbs Brewery in Aberbeeg to become its Managing Director, a position that he held for 18 years. His expansion programme there included the acquisition of the Rhondda Breweries and two cider works. A profitable scheme that he introduced at Webbs was to offer low-cost loans to Workingmen's Clubs throughout the valleys on the understanding that the Clubs sold only Webbs beer.

William Cox was the eldest of 10 children and the only one to remain in Wales whilst his entire family returned to Scotland to live. He learned about the licensing trade when his father ran the Royal Oak pub for some years at Llanwenarth. He joined Andrew Buchans in November 1901 and retired in 1931. His penchant for spotting good tenants kept him in close touch with public houses where he could often troubleshoot and identify pubs that had underperformed.

Ronald Cox, his son, was the only one of ten children to have worked in the Brewery from the age of 13. He studied through evening classes and correspondence courses to qualify as an accountant and when Bill Jones left to join Webbs in 1942, was appointed as Secretary and Accountant of the Brewery. He was appointed a Director in 1952 and achieved the distinction of being the only Rhymney member of the Board in its independent years. Ron Cox retired in 1969 after 53 years service with Andrew Buchans.

By the year 1924 there were over a hundred employees at Rhymney under the management of GL Pares MA and the document here shows a full list of the workforce from administrators to manual workers.

Malted barley delivered to the Mill House had to be crushed in the mill into a coarse flour prior to washing. The ground malt was then mixed with hot water in the grist hopper where the starch was broken down into fermentable sugars. The extract was then drawn off as wort in the Mash Tun.

A sack of malted barley, brought in by rail from Norfolk is taken to the mill for crushing.

Seen here is Thomas Edwards removing spent grain from the Mash Tun after the extraction of the wort had taken place. Spent grain was usually given free to local farmers who fed it to their cattle. Extra portions could be obtained by offering a 'back-hander' to the brewery worker involved, 'a few bob as a tip' being secreted in a matchbox which would have been lowered down from the Mash House to the farmer below.

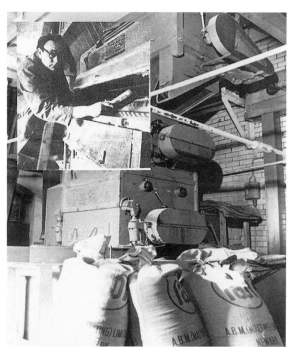

Len Ward (inset) worked in the Malthouse Screen and Mill where the newly delivered barley malt was washed and crushed.

Bill Dallimore (inset left) worked for the Brewery for 40 years until 1978 where he became a foreman and was responsible for checking the brew on its journey to the Mash Tun. He lived at nearby Tre-Edwards. Inset on the right Steve Pritchard checks the temperature of the Mash Tun. Assistant brewer Pritchard started working in the Rhymney Brewery in 1958 before which he was employed at Ely Brewery, Cardiff where his father was Head Brewer. One of the changes at Rhymney that made his life easier was the introduction of stainless steel tanks called 'vessels' instead of 'copper vats'. Mr Pritchard lived for 20 years at Ty Mawr House which adjoined the rear of the Brewery, before returning to Cardiff on retirement.

This is a younger Bill Dallimore sampling for gravity in the fermenting Room.

Ralph Smith, a foreman in fermentation, adds hops to the brew in No.1 Copper in an early fermentation process. The sweet wort produced is subsequently boiled with the addition of hops to produce a bitter hopped wort. Boiling also helps to remove unwanted ingredients which could produce a haze in the finished brew. After boiling, the beer is pumped through a cooler on its way to the fermenting vessel which was originally made of copper.

This was the Brewery's Yeast Room which contained the collection vessels and filter presses. Yeast is added to the brew to ferment the wort and convert the sugar to alcohol.

Here in No.2 Fermentation Room, Sid Pearce, brew house foreman tests the brew. After initial fermentation the beer is moved to storage tanks where a secondary fermentation takes place, giving the beer its sparkle. After filtering and the addition of carbon dioxide, the beer is ready for bottling or kegging.

The finished product is pumped into barrels, on this occasion by Trevor White, Mr Smith and Bobby Meade. During its lifetime 7 million barrels of beer were rolled out of the Rhymney Brewery until its closure on 27th April 1978. Inset is John Edwards the 'wort runner', checking the temperature of the flow of liquid.

Here we see John Morgan, Edwin Jones, Clary Burton and John Williams in 1951 in the process of loading up filled barrels for delivery.

This was the Brewery's draught beer cellar No.4 where final checking was carried out on the conveyor. Inset left are Gwyn Price, Brian Morgan and Ken Gardner inspecting the casks. On the right is Joe Fletcher the Production Manager.

This is the ground floor cask yard with cask inspection being undertaken. Inset is Elvet Jones of Upper Ras Bryn Oer Farm who was employed there. The barrels/casks were from here transported to the 'White City' (so-called because of its white-washed walls and cleanliness) where the 'finings' were added before being sent for re-filling. The 'Blow Off' area was the section of the Brewery where returned barrels/casks were washed for re-use. It incorporated a washing machine through which the barrels were hoisted and tracked for filling with boiling water. To check the quality of the cleansing, a 'sniffer' would use a flame from a copper rod, insert it into the barrel and then smell any odours that were exuded. He could tell from experience the exact state of the cleanliness of the barrel.

The Brewery Yard stocked with barrels ready for pick-up and delivery.

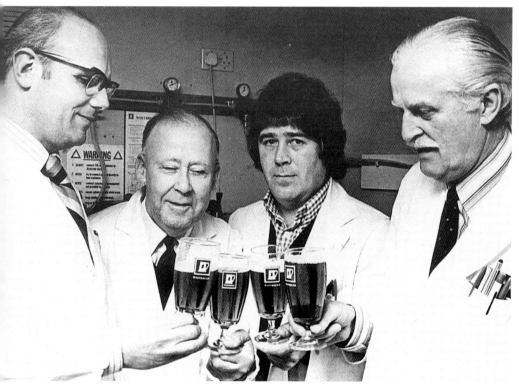

'our brewers try out the product in their Sample Room when the Brewery became Vhitbread Wales. They are John Smith, Steve Pritchard, Brian Brown and Alan Milinar.

A *wide variety of training and apprenticeships were given at Rhymney Brewery to develop the many skills required in the brewing industry. This is the cooperage, where with his specialised tools, the cooper carried out each process of his trade skilfully and with great care in order that the Brewery's product could be delivered safely and hygienically to the customer. Busily engaged are Jim Trunks and Neville Davies.*

Seen here is Mr Len Ward, a skilled cooper who worked in the Brewery for 33 years. Coopers completed a five-year apprenticeship in the making and repairing of wooden vessels. There are three classes of coopering - dry, white and wet. Brewery coopers undertook wet coopering to make barrels that were to hold liquid, the most skilful and exacting of the three. In earlier days they made use of rushes for their hygroscopic, moisture-absorbing qualities to maintain a water-tight joint between the staves of the barrel. They utilised a 'Flagging Iron' to insert the rushes when repairing leaking barrels and the process was called 'Chiming the Flags'. The more up-to-date hemp cord was later used for sealing purposes. Coopering came to an end at Rhymney in 1963 with the introduction of metal containers.

Ralph Williams of Garden City loads and unloads from the store with his forklift truck while working with Rhymney Brewery. He has vivid memories of Roddy Llewellyn, the son of Lt. Col. Harry Llewellyn, being given rides on his truck, when as a child, he used to visit with his father. Also in the photograph is Bob Phillips the foreman of Garden City.

This was the input end of the bottle-washing plant at the Brewery.

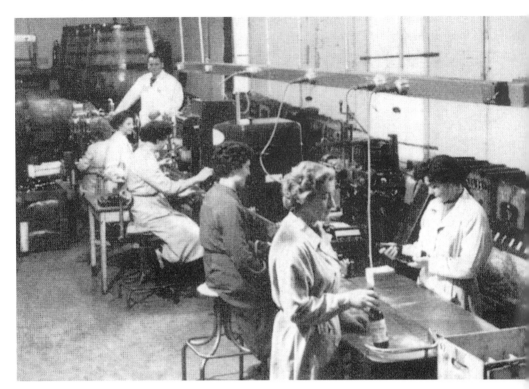

This was the bottling plant in the wine and spirits department and in the background can be seen a huge spirit cask which contained sufficient to fill 1,800 bottles.

Pictured here is the important labelling machine in the soft drinks department.

The draymen from the era of the dray horse to that of the pressurised wagon, travelled far and wide in all weathers to deliver the goods. Pictured here is Harold Davies and his mate making a delivery to the Royal Hotel, Rhymney in the depths of winter.

This is the board of Rhymney Breweries Ltd when Harry Llewellyn was Chairman there. From the left were NWG Taylor DSC, JM Skillington, Capt. Mason H Scott RN (ret'd), PW Kemp-Welch OBE (vice-chairman), Lt Col HM Llewellyn CBE JP (chairman), DR Cox (secretary), JE Martineau and MF Jupp.

One of the blacksmiths employed by Rhymney Brewery was a Mr B.Jenkins shown above, who it is understood was an uncle to the well-known Rhymney poet Idris Davies. In his day, Mr Jenkins would have been visited by callers requesting a bottle of the water in which he had cooled his red-hot horseshoes. It was a well-known fact that the ferrous water residue was a sure cure for warts!

A group of draymen get together outside the 'lapping room' to enjoy their daily 'pinta'. Among those to be seen are Harry Saunders, Mr Williams, Mrs Grower and Carl Barnard.

'Lapping' was a tradition in the Brewery that dated back countless years and it meant that employees were entitled to two free pints of beer a day and to an extra pint whenever overtime was worked. The 'Lapping Room' at Rhymney Brewery, where morning and afternoon drinks were taken had become a focal point since the Brewery's inception in 1839 and gathering there was a pleasant daily social event. Unfortunately all this had to come to an end for the Transport Department in 1963, when it was decided by the Health and Safety Committee of the Brewery that drinking and driving could be hazardous and that 'lapping' should cease forthwith. Instead, those affected were given checks which could be used in the nearby Farmers Arms. The internal fork-lift section was also declared 'dry' and workers there were allowed a 'home allowance' instead. To suitably recognise the last 'lapping day' the Depot Manager, Neville Root invited Jack English, a retired employee aged 71, who had worked with the Brewery for 51 years, to a celebration to mark the event. In this photograph and suitably armed are, left to right, Ron Magness who

served 24 years with the Company, Jack English - Distribution Supervisor, David Morgan and Neville Root.

CHAPTER 9
The Product

Rhymney's beers have always held the public's favour because of the eminent quality of the water used, the Company's purchasing acumen, their technical expertise and their first-class storage facilities. Throughout the years their product has been highly esteemed and they have been awarded many prize medals for their beers.

Some of the medals that have been awarded to the Brewery for the quality of their product. At the National Brewers Exhibition in 1888 held in London, Andrew Buchan & Co. was awarded a Silver Medal for their Old Beer and a Bronze Medal for their Stout.

By the same token, the Brewery also awarded medals to its workers for their long service and loyalty to the Company. In 1908 it was decided by the Board to award employees with 20 years service or more; many such awards were made and records show that a number of employees had as much as 45, 50 and 53 years with the Company. The particular medal seen in this photograph was awarded to David Benjamin Jones (known as 'DB'), who was the father of Tom Jones CH, author of 'Rhymney Memories' and the grandfather of Dame Eirene White. The reverse of the medal is inscribed 'Presented to DB Jones for 20 years good and faithful service. January 6th 1909.

Mr Nick Redman, the Company Archivist for Whitbread plc came to Rhymney in 1992 to research information which he sought for the Company's newsletter. He is seen here holding another long-service medal which is on display at the Whitbread Archive in Chiswell Street, London.

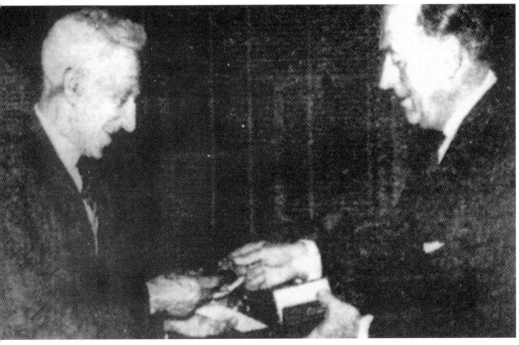

The longest serving employee of the Brewery was Sid Allen who retired in 1963 after 56 years with the Company, spanning the days of dray-horses and steam and petrol-driven wagons. He is pictured here receiving a gold watch from company Chairman Lt. Col. Harry Llewellyn at the Rhymney Breweries canteen in Cardiff where 141 awards were made. Amazingly Sid remained teetotal throughout his life.

Jack English, Bill 'the pop', George Rogers, Ben Brean, Morgan Young, Eddie Powell and Bill 'WC' Jones all drivers with the Brewery enjoy a pint at the Farmers Arms following an awards presentation.

The above brass plaque which is retained in the Whitbread Archives, London lists in 1908 those workers with 20 years service with Buchan's Brewery. It reads - 'The undersigned have been presented with silver medals in recognition of 20 years good and faithful service with the Company. Thomas Edwards, Manager'. Those listed are: Thomas Edwards, John Maddocks, Alfred Stockwell, William Burrell, John Garfield, Nathaniel Pullin, James Jones, Morgan Jordan, David Benjamin Jones, William Griffiths, Mrs Sarah Price, David Bevan, Thomas Williams, William Hughes.

A selection of the Brewery's products over the years were well-publicised on beer mats throughout the locality.

A multitude of relics from the Rhymney Brewery, including a bottle opener and an array of advertising devices such as beer mats, trays, ash trays, bottle labels and posters are displayed behind glass at the Whitbread Archive Museum, London. On Whitbread's closure, its Company Archivist Nick Redman deposited their artefacts in a number of locations.

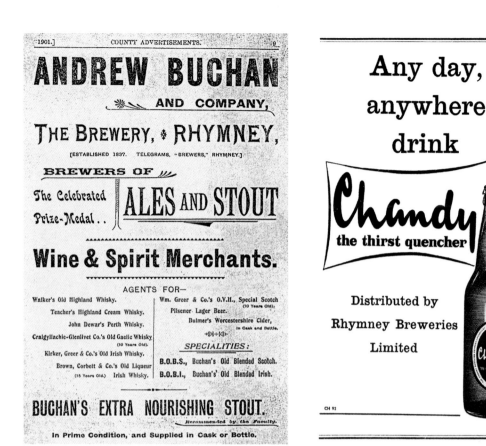

Newspaper advertisements were widely used by the Brewery, one of which seen here shows that Andrew Buchan's also served as agents for the sale of a variety of Scottish and Irish Whiskies, Pilsener Lager and Bulmer's Cider. They also bottled the very popular 'Chandy'. Every opportunity was taken to promote their products such as the advertisement on Tramcar No.8 seen at Merthyr Tydfil Depot and a wide variety of useful implements.

CHAPTER 10

Buchan's Estate

In 1939 Andrew Buchan's Breweries and Associated Companies held a total of 362 hotels and inns, all of which can be seen listed below and on the following page.

THE HOTELS AND INNS
of
ANDREW BUCHAN'S BREWERIES AND ASSOCIATED COMPANIES

RHYMNEY
Royal Hotel
Castle Hotel
Queen's Hotel
Farmers Arms
Puddlers Arms
Penywaun Hotel
Tredegar Arms
Clarence Inn

RHYMNEY BRIDGE
Beaufort Arms

BUTETOWN
Windsor Arms

PONTLOTTYN
Railway Inn
Blast Furnace Hotel
General Picton Hotel
Lord Nelson Inn

ABERTYSSWG
Mountain Ash Inn

TIRPHIL
Rising Sun Inn

CWMSIFIOG
Queen's Hotel

ABERBARGOED
Travellers Rest
Smiths Arms
Greyhound Inn

BARGOED
Old Mill Hotel
Royal Hotel

FOCHRIW
White Horse Inn

DERI
Bailey's Arms

PENGAM
Half Way Hotel
Ivybush Hotel
Smiths Arms
Trelyn Hotel
Tredegar Arms
Gwerthoner Hotel

GELLYGAER
Harp Inn

FLEUR DE LYS
New Inn

MAESYCWMMER
Maesycwmmer Inn

PENALLTA
Fox and Hounds

YSTRADMYNACH
Coopers Arms
Beech Tree Hotel

LLANBRADACH
De Winton Hotel
Wingfield Hotel

CAERPHILLY
Masons Arms
Station Inn
Pontygwindy Inn
Castle Hotel
Goodrich Hotel
Blue Bell Inn

BEDWAS
Royal Oak Inn
Church House Inn
Fishermen's Rest

MACHEN
White Hart Inn
Royal Oak Inn
Tredegar Arms

GROESWEN
White Cross Inn

ABERTRIDWR
Panteg Hotel

PENYRHEOL (CAERPHILLY)
Angel Inn

SENGHENYDD
Universal Hotel

TAFARNAUBACH
Prince of Wales
Travellers Rest

TREDEGAR
Coach and Horses
North Western Hotel
George Hotel
Red Lion Inn
King's Head Inn
Golden Lion Inn
Greyhound Hotel
Britannia Inn
Freemasons Inn
Castle Hotel

DUKESTOWN
Rising Sun Inn
Prince Llewellyn Inn
Queen Victoria Inn
Belle Vue Inn
Star Inn

TREVIL
Quarrymen's Arms
Castle Inn

HOLLYBUSH
Ancient Druid Inn

BEDWELLTY
Church Inn
New Inn

BLACKWOOD
Royal Oak Inn
Rock Inn
Parrot Inn
Crown Inn

BLACKWOOD—*continued*
Tredegar Arms
Butchers Arms
Masons Arms
Foresters' Arms

OAKDALE
Oakdale Hotel

PENMAEN
Ivybush Inn
Cross Oak Inn

PONTLLANFRAITH
Tredegar Junction Hotel
Ivor Arms
Prince of Wales

GELLIGROES
Half Way House

PENTWYNMAWR
Three Horse Shoes

NEWBRIDGE
Red Lion Inn

YNYSDDU
Black Prince Inn
Pioneer Hotel

MYNYDDISLWYN
Church Inn

ARGOED
Argoed Arms

BEAUFORT
Rising Sun Inn
Beaufort Inn
Cross Keys Inn

BRYNMAWR
King William IV Inn
Swan Inn
King's Head Inn
Railway Inn
New Griffin Inn
Clarence Inn
Royal Arms
White Lion Inn
Rising Sun Inn
Golddiggers Hotel
Belle Vue Hotel

NANTYGLO
Firemen's Arms
Golden Lion Inn
Vine Inn

BLAINA
Royal Exchange Inn
King's Head Inn
Lamb Inn
Rolling Mill Inn
Ballers Arms
Miners Arms

ABERBEEG
Carpenters Arms

EBBW VALE
Britannia Inn
Duke of Wellington Inn
Heolymwyn Inn
King's Arms
Lamb Inn

VICTORIA
Bush Inn

CWM
Bailey's Arms

CRUMLIN
Bridgend Inn
Railway Inn
Masons Arms
Viaduct Tavern

ABERCARN
Commercial Hotel

RISCA
Bridgend Inn

ROGERSTONE
Tydu Hotel

NEWPORT
Black Swan Inn
Railway Inn
Fair Oak Inn
Hope Inn
Ship Hotel
Mechanics Arms

CWMBRAN
Railway Inn

HENLLYS
Castell-y-Bwch Inn

GOYTREY
Goytrey Arms

USK
Castle Hotel
Golden Lion Hotel
Cross Keys Inn
Gate Inn, Llanfrechfa

WHITCHURCH
Crown Hotel

GILWERN
Five Bells Inn
Forge Hammer Inn
Bridgend Inn

CLYDACH
Hafod Inn

ABERGAVENNY
White Horse Inn
London Hotel

LLANGYNIDR
Beaufort Arms

BLAENAVON
Railway Hotel
New King's Arms
Royal Exchange Inn
Foresters Arms
Oxford Inn
White Hart Inn
Castle Hotel
Ivor Restaurant
Prince of Wales Inn
Waun Tavern
Golden Boot Inn
Swan Inn
Belle Vue Inn
Rising Sun Inn
Three Cranes Inn
King's Arms
Rock and Fountain Inn
Riflemen's Arms

Many of the Brewery's local pubs and hotels still exist today but some, such as the Wellington Arms, The Cyclops, The Railway Inn (Pontlottyn) and a number of Clubs that were Brewery customers have long since been demolished. Each house over the years has involved itself in sporting and social activities which were very often supported by the Brewery and some of these activities are shown amidst the following pages with the pub or hotel concerned.

One of the oldest inns in Rhymney (still in existence today as a private residence) was the Beaufort Arms at Rhymney Bridge which has also been called the Rhymney Inn. Mr David Thomas is standing next to his Austin Seven.

The Badminton Papers, held in Aberystwyth, contain an old map dated 1780 which indicates the presence of a large house, several smaller houses and a few surrounding farms in the vicinity of Rhymney Bridge. Further records show that a meeting of craftsmen was held at the Beaufort Arms, Rhymney Bridge which Richard Crawshay and Benjamin Hall both attended. During and before the time that this pre-1780 inn became a holding of Andrew Buchan's Brewery, it was a regular stopping place for coachmen making their way through the Rhymney Bridge toll-gate on this important east to west line of communication. Until 1807 the Baptists, Independents and Calvinistic Methodists had worshipped in private houses. This was when a Mr Overton, the surveyor and engineer responsible for the construction of the Bryn Oer Tramway, persuaded them to meet and worship together at the Beaufort Arms. A pulpit chair was acquired from Blackwood and was used for some time at the tavern before eventually finding its way to Graig Chapel. Unfortunately this tripartite arrangement did not last because of disagreements over the leasing and the Baptists and Independents reverted to cottage worship until their individual chapels were built.

In 1841 the proprietor of the Beaufort Arms was a Joseph Hancock. The preceding photograph shows the inn during the 1920s with a Mr David Thomas proudly standing alongside his Austin Seven motor car. Mr Thomas was born in Talgarth in 1870, a carpenter by trade who came to Rhymney in 1918 to work as a Supervisory Architect at the Andrew Buchan Brewery.

The Castle Hotel, Rhymney another of Buchan's holdings.

The Castle was built in 1842 by Morgan Morgan who came from Castle Manor, Brecon from which he named the inn. In 1857 his four sons emigrated to Australia in order to prospect for gold. They initially worked at the Deep Lead goldfield near Stawell and from there they took up a mining claim at Moyston which proved to be very successful for them. Considerable excitement was to prevail in the town owing to the report of the discovery of a rich gold-bearing reef by Morgan J Morgan and his brother William'. The claim was situated about 12 miles north of Ararat and the Morgan brothers named it Rhymney Reef after their home town and since then the district has been known as Rhymney Reef or Rhymney. It was also a well-known wine-producing area. Hotels and inns were the frequent meeting places of various societies and clubs and the Castle Hotel, in its early days, housed the Owain Glyndwr Lodge which was the Rhymney Ivorian Section of the Oddfellows Friendly Society. Such societies were set up to help, as best they could, the poor and needy in the area, usually financially supported by subscriptions from its members. The Castle was also used as the headquarters for local sporting activities such as shooting clubs and cricket and football teams.

The Penydre United football team had their headquarters at the Castle Hotel wher they changed into kit before playing at The Track football ground. The team wa formed in 1950 by ME Llewellyn and B Price and they won the Rhymney Valle League Cup on the first time they entered the competition. They were also winner of the Rhymney Valley Victory Cup and were undefeated throughout the seasor. Included in this photograph are - G Evans, D Moon, TH Davies, E Price, I Price T Thomas, D Williams, W Carroll, T Rees, L Goode and J Zeraschi; Mr A William (President), E Llewellyn (Chairman), F Harris (Secretary) and D Newell.

Malcolm Cox, an ex-employee c Rhymney Brewery, together wit Dr Richard Evans point ou the Rhymney signpost c Shea's Flat in Rhymney Ree Australia. This is the site of th township near the gold rus which started in the area i 1865 and which formed th origins of Rhymney.

The Penywaun Hotel which stood in Upper High Street, Rhymney also had its fair share of society meetings and social and sporting activities within its walls. Inset are its proprietors in the 1950s Mr and Mrs Albert Williams.

This gathering in the Penywaun Hotel was the annual awards night in 1950 of the Rhymney Amateur Football Club where its Chairman Maynard Brown is making a presentation. Among those present are David Sutton, Eddie 'Tonddu' Williams, Harold Keddle, Davis Jones 'Shegaer' and David Vaughan.

The Queen Victoria Hotel, also known as 'The Queens' was situated next to Cwm Shon Matthews Square and has long been demolished. Here we see the original Fochriw Mini Paraders Jazz Band marching smartly past the hotel in the 1969 carnival. Six years later the Mini Paraders brought tremendous prestige to Fochriw by becoming World Champions at an international competition held in Porthcawl.

The award-winning Rhymney Miners Piped Band display their trophies at the rear of the Queen Victoria Hotel, their headquarters, in 1926 with their pipes, drums and miners' lamps very much in evidence. It will be seen that 'The Queens' was indisputably a Buchan house. Inset, right is what remained of the old original Queen Victoria Inn in 1978, then a private dwelling. The old 'Vic' was situated at the end of Jenkins Row near the top end of Lady Tyler Terrace which was originally called Pond Row and Rowles Square.

VISITORS TO RHYMNEY . . .

On WHIT-TUESDAY

Will find every Accommodation at the

Royal Arms Hotel.

Large BANQUETING ROOM

Where CHOIRS and PARTIES can be Provided
with LUNCHEON, &c. at Short Notice.

Sandwiches, -
Cold Luncheons,

AND ALL KINDS OF

. . . Refreshments.

BUCHAN'S . . .
Celebrated "KING'S ALE."

A. M. DAVIES, Proprietress.

Another Buchan's holding and once the purveyors of Buchan's Celebrated King's Ale, the Royal Arms Hotel still trades at the Royal Square in Rhymney. Once an important meeting place where Inquests and Assizes were held, some of its previous proprietors were, in 1852 Sarah Morgan, in 1862 John Davies to be followed in the same year by Jayne Cross. The Rhymney and Pontlottyn Chamber of Trade held their meetings there and in 1900 were invited by the Railway company to shut up shop and to join an excursion to Ilfracombe that they had put on - a trip that had regularly taken place for the last 30 years. The traders however, much disgruntled by the idea of losing money by tripping on a working day instead of on the usual weekend, flatly turned the offer down. They decided instead to arrange their own excursion by charabanc to Tintern Abbey and Chepstow!

A charabanc full to the brim with excursionists leaves the Royal Arms Hotel for, no doubt, an eventful day out. Seats were in rows of six and the vehicle held up to 34 passengers. It had a large convertible hood at the back and they were given such names as 'The Rhymney Rambler', 'The White Hope' and 'The Bluebird'.

For many years the Royal Hotel has been the headquarters of the Rhymney Royal Bowling Club who, in 2006, became the Monmouthshire Bowling Association' Third Division Champions. The team shown here from left to right were - Back K Bartlett, N Protheroe, J Watkins, C O'Brien, A Jenkins and R Roberts. Middle J Doyle, D Hann, R Withers, I Prosser, R Williams and T O'Brien. Front: G Elias D Morgan, N James, A James, P Cosh and P White.

The Farmers Arms, Rhymney built in 1875 has always been a favourite stopping-o point for brewery workers on their way home from work. Originally a farmhous known as Ty Elwir, it was later to become part of the estate of the Andrew Bucha brewing empire. It was also a centre for sporting and social activities and particula mention must be made of their 'Farmer Lilies' rugby football team established c the first village team in 1900. Well-documented for its achievements and for th enthusiasm of its members, it had its base for many years at the 'Farmers' whil playing its matches at the Nantllesg football pitch. A long-gone previous tenant, Mrs Willis is still said to make her presence known in ghostly fashion at the inn an to have freely communicated from the grave with its later residents.

Elated supporters of the Welsh rugby team congregate outside the Farmers Arms in 1971 before leaving for Murrayfield. Among the group are to be seen Jack Patten, Harry Wharton, Idris Jones 'The Laundry', Arthur Simpson, Benny Jones, Reg Roberts, Huw Griffiths, John Griffiths, Dick Roberts, Dale Jones, Roy Williams, Maynard Theophilus, Bill 'Scouse' Jones, Lyn Owen, Dai 'Reb' Jones, Reg Davies, Ken Morgan, Billy Rees, Cecil Darlington. Dai Jones 'Brewery Club', Bob Jones, Edgerton White, John Coonick, Alan John, Glan Greening, Sid Prosser, Ken Evans, Thomas Henry Davies, Billy Phillips, Alan Jones, Harry Cavender, Cyril Phillips, Gwyn 'The Baron' Thomas and Terry Tapscott.

The McLaren Amateur Football Team, Abertysswg, had their headquarters in the McLaren Arms and here we see their 1961-62 team. Pictured on The Green, Abertysswg are C May, J Norris, P Isaac, W May (Secretary), W Stockman, B Dufty, A Morgan, B Jones, J Morris, G Powell, C Jones, C Crane, F May, K Jones, G Stockman, R Withers, K Lloyd, S Lloyd, J Evans, A Lloyd and J Baker.

This is an intriguing old photograph of the Quarryman's Arms, Trefil, grandly displaying its Andrew Buchan & Co. 'Prize Medal Ale and Stout' sign. Sitting in the trap is a Mr Rake who ran an auctioneering concern in Church Street, Tredegar. The inn was originally a private dwelling known as Ty Uchaf (Top House) and is now the Mountain Air Inn. An early landlord was Richard Samuel who later became the owner of Bryn Bach Farm.

The Windsor Arms was built as a house with the rest of Bute Town in the 1820s. Converted into an inn, its early proprietors in 1858 were Daniel and Phoebe Davies. Here, with its Andrew Buchan sign clearly in evidence we see its proprietor in around 1878, Rees Harris, the grandfather of Mr R Harris who also lived in the village all of his life.

The committee of the Windsor Arms Football Club in 1980 consisted of, at the back, left to right: J Matthews (Fixture Secretary), N Davies (Secretary), S Matthews (Treasurer), N Davies (Manager B), D Moseley, M Thomas (Manager A), G Morgan (Club Captain). In the front row are L Oakley, Albert Morgan (Chairman), J Griffiths (President), I Jones (Life Member) and N Pickett (Vice Chairman).

The Puddlers Arms earned its name from the early process of 'puddling' in the production of pig iron, later replaced by the improved Bessemer process. Puddlers were responsible for continually stirring the molten iron with iron bars to ensure separation from the slag and other impurities and to maintain an even quality. The work was hot and dangerous and puddlers could be identified by the sallowness of their complexion caused by the heat of the furnace.

The Lord Nelson Inn, Pontlottyn, named after the great Admiral himself displays its Andrew Buchan's 'Celebrated Prize Medal Ales and Stout' sign in 1914 when Morris Davies was its proprietor. Other proprietors were, in 1875 Moses Thomas; in 1898 DB Bowen who died in 1906; in 1920 Alfred Prosser who died when returning from Hereford in a charabanc.

The Clarence Inn, Rhymney, here embellished by the 'Hobby Horse', was built in the early 1800s and witnessed the many trials and tribulations that the 'Old Rhymney' experienced in her tough upbringing. A focal point for a wide range of activities, The Clarence in its earlier years played host to the Philanthropic Order of the True Ivorites, which was a Welsh language order founded in 1836 whose President and Grand Master of the time was Brother Enoch James and its secretary Thomas Thomas. Their host was Councillor Benjamin Rees who was manager of the inn for 23 years but who died in most unusual circumstances when he drowned in 21 inches of water in a well in the cellar of the inn when fetching beer.

This is the ladies' darts team of the Clarence Inn which was transferred to the Three Counties Hotel on its closure. This was in 1973 when they played in the Rhymney and Tredegar District Ladies Darts League. In the back row, from left to right are Betty Trowbridge, Estelle (Brooks) Trowbridge, Marie Edwards, Dai 'The Post' Williams who presented their trophies, Alyson Thomas, Lilian Evans, Elythia Jones and Mary Griffiths. In the front are Edith Davies, Alice Williams, Ethel Pat Minhinnick, Marion Thomas and Patricia Williams.

The Blast Furnace Inn, Pontlottyn, shown when it was a house of the Rhymney Crosswell Brewery which at one time ran its own brew house - an attached 14-barrel plant. Jenkin Edwards owned the building as a farmhouse in 1825 and later converted it to an alehouse 'to help quench local thirsts'.

One of the many teams of the Pontlottyn Blast Furnace Football Club displays its trophies after a successful season. In the back row, from left to right are to be seen: Dai Moseley, Ken Jones, John Oakley, Idwal Price, Philip Jones, Keith Jones, Mike McGhee, Tyrone Bradbeer, Steve Herbert and Raynard Carey. In the middle are: David Evans, Ian Ross, Terence O'Brien, Jeff Webber, Peter Radford, Robin Crane, Mal Bradbeer, Jeffrey Griffiths, Gwyn Evans, Malcolm Diggle, Merlin Davies and David Morgan. In front are Peter Lloyd, John Dufty, Alan (Chunky) James, Mike (Darky) Hughes, David Jones and Barrie Griffiths.

Members of the Princetown Club on a supporters' trip to Scotland in 1955, fly the colours outside the Rockburgh Hotel in Dunbar. Among them, from the back row, are to be seen: Ted (The Box) Williams, Islwyn Price, Charlie McMahon, David Morris, Bob Powell, Albert Oakley, Jim Moseley, John Ivor Morgan, Norris Stephens, Mr Hancock, Ivor Thomas, Dick Prosser, Billy Hancock, Les Griffiths, Johnny (Twynny) Thomas, Mr Bradley, Trevor Hancock, John Williams, Roy Taylor, Jackie Thomas, Edgar Robinson and Club Secretary Ollie Williams.

The Prince of Wales Inn, Princetown, with its distinctive 'Hobby Horse' sign, was built in 1875. Here we see it when petrol and oil sales represented a part of the business there.

Abe Morgan on the right, a long serving employee of the Rhymney Brewery, and also the President of the Tredegar Mentally Handicapped Association, accepts a cheque for £500 from Johnny Owen at the Prince of Wales Inn, Princetown. A total of £600 had been collected by raffles at 'The Prince', £100 of which was donated to Homes in London. Johnny, the Merthyr boxing hero, was a good friend of the inn's proprietors 'Nick the Prince' Nicholas and his wife Irene, who are also shown here.

In Forge Street, Rhymney, opposite Moriah Street, was once situated The Cyclops Inn, a public house that was later to become a private dwelling. Its proprietor in 1852 was a Henry Jones and in 1862 a William Scott. Inns were often named from occupations in the iron industry and frequented by workers involved in such activity. The Cyclops Inn would undoubtedly have received its name from the shinglers who worked at the nearby Middle and Lower furnaces. Shinglers were the men who hammered the hot iron after it had been puddled and they were susceptible to the continuous shower of iron sparks that was thrown off. To protect themselves, a specialised leather dress covered the whole of their body, reinforced with large metal plates. Their heads were covered with a leather hood in the centre of which was a single large glass eye, completing the effigy of the mythical Cyclops from which the shinglers were to earn their nickname.

The Mountain Ash Inn, here in the hands of Rhymney and Crosswells, is still situated on the Cwmtysswg mountainside above the village of Abertysswg.

A much earlier picture of the Mountain Ash Inn when in the hands of the Buchan Estate.

The Royal Arms Hotel, at one time a house of Andrew Buchans, was built in the middle of the 19th century to serve the isolated village of Pantywaun, on the Fochriw to Dowlais mountain. Owned by the Brewery, it met its demise when, in 1962, open cast coal mining activities began in the area with the intention of completely demolishing the village. The licensee, Mrs Elsie Evans, who lived at the hotel with her husband John Thomas Evans and their six sons, held out no hope for the hotel's future. The Brewery reported that they had no definite plans but once the houses of the village were pulled down, there was no way of keeping the hotel alive and it would probably have to die along with the village.

89

In its earlier days the Travellers Rest in Tafarnaubach was a house of the Taff Vale Brewery and here it advertises its Prize Medal Beers. Built in 1851, its first manager was Thomas Morgan of Aberdare, who lived there with his wife Mary, children Jane, William and John, house servant Margaret Davies and lodger William Williams. When not drawing ale, Thomas Morgan mined the coal seams behind. The Bryn Oer Tramway at one time ran in front of the inn on its route from Trefil to the Union Ironworks at the Garn, near Rhymney Bridge.

The Tredegar Arms, Hill Street, Rhymney, a Rhymney and later Whitbread house was for many years the headquarters of the Foresters, one of the many benevolent organisations that were to be found throughout the country. Their meeting place was referred to as a 'Lodge' and each Lodge had its own individually named 'Court'. The Tredegar Arms housed the Court Maid Adeline of the Forestry Lodge and it was here on 16th August 1886, that it celebrated in fine style, its anniversary. The celebration consisted of a grand march through the town with a fellow Lodge to be followed by an evening of refreshments at the inn. Joining the Court Maid Adeline was the Jubilee Court of the Blast Furnace inn, Pontlottyn and together they set off through Rhymney headed by eighteen members on horseback dressed in Lincoln Green in the finest Robin Hood tradition. They were then wined and dined in the evening back at the 'TA', fully appreciative of the excellent results of the day's celebrations.

Clubs of various sorts, although not 'tied' to the Brewery, would avail themselves of its products and would often closely relate themselves in order to receive loans or other benefits that the Brewery may be prepared to offer. This is the Workingmen's Club on the Rhymney High Street which, before being greatly extended, was originally a small tea-house.

This is the industrious Ladies' Committee of the Rhymney Workingmen's Club who rest their feet for a well-earned break. In the back row are Mary Church, Mrs Roberts, Phyllis Crowley, Laura Lloyd, Marlene Richards, Ann Roberts, Anita Howells and Aggie Jones. Amongst the seated are Nancy Rees, Evelyn Hanley, Barbara Hook and Hetty Eynon.

A busload of happy supporters on their way from the Workingmen's Club to Ireland prepare to embark for the 1950 international match. Among the group are to be seen Enoch Rist, Gwyn Jones (Tai Level Lo), Eddie Jenkins, Handel Meyrick, Matthew (Tai Bach), Jackie Gardener (Red House Row), Alan Rist, Will Davies (Ty'lan) Harry Williams (Talybont), Ken Gardener and Eddie (Ty'lan) Davies.

Another much earlier trip for Workmen's Club members, this time by charabanc for the Farmers' Section in their 'Victory Car'.

Rhymney's first Constitutional Club was housed in Mount Pleasant in a building that had originally been the local base of the Salvation Army. Reportedly haunted by a lady in grey costume and bonnet, it is said that she was a returning Salvation Army member unable to rest because of the ungodly levels of drinking and revelry that were taking place in her once haven of peace.

Some of the members of the 'Connie Club' in the 1950s were: Johnny Rowlands, Terry (Dixie Lee) Williams , Billy Rowlands, Dai Francis, Percy Jones and Jackie Collins.

A much earlier façade of the Constitutional Club, taken when John Hennessey was its steward. Here we see his grandchildren Derek Hennessey with sister Georgina, known as Gene, posing outside the Club.

Rhymney Brewery holdings extended throughout South Wales and over the English border and 'where the Hobby Horse Roams' since its inception in 1930, became the Brewery's signature tune for the pubs and hotels within its territory. Space does not allow the showing of every individual public house or hotel outside the immediate local area so a carefully prepared cross section of those that appear visually the most interesting are recorded in the following pages.

The fascinating Fountain Inn, also known as 'The Farm' was a converted farmhouse in Troedrhiwgwair, a very small village below Tredegar. With its stone tiled roof and mother nursing her baby 'Welsh fashion' in the shawl, it captures a moment that must be preserved. The landlord at the time, Alfred Thomas is believed to have dealt with the Andrew Buchan Brewery and here he is seen with his two border collies.

The Coopers Arms in Ystrad Mynach.

The White Horse Inn in Fochriw.

The Rhyd Hall in Tredegar.

The Goytre Arms near Pontypool.

'he Forge Hammer Inn in Gilwern near Abergavenny.

The Fox and Hounds, Penallta.

'he Prince Llewellyn Inn in Dukestown, Tredegar.

The Church Inn Bedwellty.

A superb picture of the Troedrhiw Fuwch Inn in 1887 and a more recent one in 196?
showing landlady Mrs N Morgan with her sister Mrs A Roberts at the bar. The inn
was a focal point for the village and it has a rich history.

The Castle Hotel, Usk.

The Blue Bell Inn, St. Mellons.

The Glamorgan Arms, Abercanaid.

The Tanyard Arms, Merthyr Tydfil.

The Clarence Hotel, Maesteg.

The Patriot Inn, Dowlais.

The Old Angel, Merthyr Tydfil.

The Dowlais Inn, Dowlais.

The Old House, Llangynwyd.

The Volunteer Arms, Merthyr Tydfil.

The Farmers Arms, Twynyrodyn, Merthyr Tydfil.

The Red Bull Inn, Merthyr Tydfil.

The New Inn, Bedwellty.

The Cross Keys Inn, Usk.

The Ivy Bush, Pengam.

The Mount Pleasant Inn, Dowlais.

The Market Tavern, Abergavenny.

The Baileys Arms Hotel, Pentre.

The Skirrid Mountain Inn at Llanvihangel Crucorney.

The Crystal Palace Inn, Penydarren, Merthyr Tydfil.

The Mardy Hotel, Merthyr Tydfil.

The Star Inn, Dukestown, Tredegar.

The Plough Inn, Penydarren, Merthyr Tydfil.

The Red Lion Hotel, Llangorse.

The Penydarren Inn, Merthyr Tydfil.

The Victoria Inn, Quakers Yard.

The Rhydfelin Inn, Rhydfelin.

The Rose and Crown, Cwmfelin.

The Greenmeadow Inn, Rudry.

The Crown Hotel, Merthyr Tydfil.

The Ty Du Hotel, Rogerstone.

Ye Olde Salutation Inn in Weobley, Herefordshire.

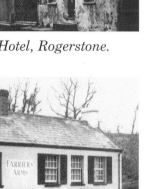

The Farriers Arms, Cwmbach.

The Snatchwood Inn, Abersychan, near Pontypool.

The North Western Hotel, Tredegar.

The Ffaldcaiach Inn, Trelewis.

The Travellers Rest, Abercynon, near Aberdare.

The Globe Inn, Tredegar.

Inn signs date back to Roman times when their taverns would be distinguished by a placard depicting a bush of vine leaves. It was a time of high illiteracy when tradesmen of all descriptions would publicise their wares with boards and signs indicating what they sold. Public houses, inns and hotels today have continued the practice but varied their depictions and instead, display signs that show famous people and historical symbols.

The very earliest inns in the country were built to accommodate pilgrims and travellers and many that were constructed near abbeys, displayed religious signs which are still to be seen today. The Crossed Keys for example was an insignia of St. Peter; The Lamb referred to Jesus Christ; The Bull to a monastic seal; The George became a corruption of St. George and The Dragon and The Lamb and Flag was from the Court of Arms of the Knights Templars indicating The Lamb of God.

Royal depictions were popular, such as a wild boar which was the crest of Richard III; the Blue Boar belonged to the crest of the Earl of Oxford who supported Henry Tudor. The Crown sign was used for inns that stood on royal property and The Lion was a common element on the Court of Arms of most Kings of England. Edward III used The Rising Sun on his crest, which has been made use of on inn signs and when he claimed the French throne, the Fleur-de-Lys became very much in evidence. This was sometimes altered to a plume of feathers when Edward's son, The Black Prince, adopted the feathers on his badge. During the occasion of the reign of Charles I, The Royal Oak became a popular sign, commemorating as it did, his escape from the Parliament Army when he hid in an oak tree at Boscobel. The White Horse is a Saxon emblem brought across by the Hanoverians.

Inns and taverns on royal lands indicated their allegiance to the Crown, while those on Manorial lands supported the local baron with their signs. Others displayed unrelated signs. Some examples are as follows: The Red Lion - John of Gaunt; The Swan - The Duke of Buckingham; The White Horse - The Earls of Arundel; The Bear - The Earls of Warwick and Leicester but also when bear-baiting took place in the tavern yard; The Bird in Hand - an indication of hawking taking place; The Nag's Head - a place where costermongers and travellers stopped; The Pelican - a symbol for the Virgin Mary; Fighting Cocks - a tavern where cock fighting took place; The Boot - said to be derived from Sir John Shorn who, in the 13th century, claimed to have conjured the Devil into a boot; The Coach and Horses - clearly a stopping-off place for stagecoaches.

The hundreds of public houses and hotels in the Rhymney Brewery's estate that depicted their own personal signs, expose a wealth of historical association. Names such as the Forge Hammer Inn in Gilwern, The Navigation Hotel in Abercynon, The Fisherman's Rest in Bedwas, The Ancient Druid Inn in Hollybush, The Volunteers Arms in Merthyr Tydfil, The Vulcan and Friendship Inn in Dowlais, The Puddlers Arms in Rhymney, The Snatchwood Inn at Abersychan and The Gold Diggers Hotel in Brynmawr are all titles to be conjured with, each with their own piece of history relating to events that were taking place at the time.

In the early 19th century it became more popular for men and some women in local industries to smoke clay pipes. These would have been bought for a farthing or obtained free from Andrew Buchan's inns and hotels. Their patterns were many and varied and, more often than not, reflected institutions and activities that were taking place at the time. Many had intricate and unusual designs while others showed the maker's name incised into the stem or his initials cut into either side of the bowl.

The author with her collection of clay pipes which were all found locally in such places as mine shafts, old and demolished buildings and old dumps.

Manufacturers imprints on the stems of pipes found locally show that Spooners of Tredegar and Havard & Son, Tredegar were both actively engaged in clay pipe making during the 19th century. Spooners' large, extensive pipe shop was built in 1847-48 at 51 Charles Street and the family seemed to have maintained the monopoly for clay-pipe making locally until 1875 when they were joined by the Havard Brothers.

Mould designing for clay-pipe manufacture was, in itself, a specialised art and masters of the craft jealously guarded the secrets of their trade. Pipes handed out to customers by hostelries and inns would often depict their own emblems such as The Prince of Wales feather, The Wellington, The Castle, The Welsh Harp, The Kings Head, The Anchor, The Cross Keys, The Lamb and Flag, The Star Inn and so on. Others were decorated purely for aesthetic reasons and would be moulded into the shapes of birds, fish, footballs and rugby balls, talons, stags' heads, often with fluted designs. The Irish influence could be seen with designs of shamrocks, the Irish harp and the shillelagh and the Scottish thistle proved a popular design as did the Welsh leek. Acorns and oak-leaves decorating pipes commemorated The Ancient Order of Druids and have been found in Rhymney, no doubt connected with their branch of the Society that gathered at the Castle Hotel.

The long-stemmed churchwarden pipes were fashionable around 1845 at the time of the Cholera plague epidemic and would have been smoked by grave-diggers and burial attendants as a means of protection against contracting the disease. People were encouraged to smoke at that time for that specific reason. Short-stemmed pipes were known as 'nose-warmers' for obvious reasons. Very small pipes, called 'fairy pipes', have also been found in plague pits, some in Rhymney.

CHAPTER 11
People and Events

Rhymney Brewery was highly regarded for its varied sports and social programmes over the years. However the period of World War Two (1939-45) proved to be an occasion when these sorts of activities took second place to the more urgent needs of the day. On the night of 14th May 1940, The Secretary of State for War, Anthony Eden, broadcast an appeal to the nation that was to stir the hearts of everyone in all the cities, towns, villages and hamlets throughout the country. The country was at war, the perilous 'Miracle of Dunkirk' was desperately taking place and invasion by German troops appeared imminent. The Regular Army was engaged in a life and death struggle with the enemy. Arms, transport and equipment had been abandoned on beaches and battlefields along the line of retreat and the country was in very serious danger. In the interests of national safety a line of defence had to be produced that would give the Regular Army breathing space in which to re-arm, re-equip and reorganise itself. The response to this appeal was immediate and the results staggering. Police Stations, Drill Halls and even garden sheds were temporarily converted into Recruiting Stations to enlist men for this new line of defence and almost overnight, a people's army was born.

Here are some members of the HQ staff of the 6th Battalion, the West Monmouthshire Section who were housed in the Rhymney Brewery during the Second World War years. Almost all Brewery employees, they additionally worked night and day in the map-filled drawing office of the Estates Department taking signalled messages and co-ordinating the activities of the Companies within the field. Training was given in telephone duties and Morse Code and practice in fire drills with stirrup pumps undertaken at the nearby brickyard. From top left are Joan (White) Howells, Olga Blake, Edwina (Price) Llewellyn and Elizabeth Williams. Central are Myra (Richards) Williams, Rene Webber, Eleanor Jones and sister Gwladys Jones, Mary Hannah Roberts, Morfydd Jones and Minnie Jones. In the front are Beryl Jenkins, Norma Kedward, Brewery Chairman Lt. Col. Hoare, Col. AJD Griffiths, Capt. Maund, Ray Thomas and Ivy Rawle.

In Rhymney the Recruitment Office and Headquarters of the Local Defence Volunteers was set up in the offices of the Rhymney Brewery under the command of Colonel JD Griffiths, backed by his second in command Lt. Col. Hoare. Housed in the drawing office of the Brewery, it was considered to be one of the better quality HQ's when compared to others elsewhere. The Rhymney community's response was remarkable and their offices were quickly besieged with recruits. So well did the Brewery serve the needs of the people's army it was subsequently adopted as the Battalion Headquarters with, initially, five Companies covering as far south as Pengam and as far east as the Sirhowy Valley. The Rhymney, Rhymney Bridge and Abertysswg districts eventually became 'A' Company of the 6th Monmouthshire Battalion Home Guard, consisting of 650 members and its establishment was to ring the death knell on its enterprising predecessor The Local Defence Volunteers.

The Home Guard, now a co-ordinated force and an integral part of the British Army, was equipped with uniforms and arms brought to the Brewery HQ by brewery lorry from the Monmouthshire TA Depot. These were delivered to the Quartermaster, a Mr Bassett and allocated to the Company Commanders by Capt. Gallop who acted as both Sector and Battalion Adjutant.

A Rhymney contingent of 'A' Company now fully uniformed and rid of their magical LDV armbands. Amongst the group are Harry Breen, Tom 'The Shop' Jones grocer of Queens Square and Billy Goode of Forge Street.

These were the men who were responsible for road blocks throughout the town, for checking identity cards, manning pill boxes and assisting in rescue work. Their exploits were sometimes serious, sometimes hilarious. The Battalion's first major alarm was on a hot Sunday in June 1940 when it was reported that five or six parachutists had been seen dropping on the Fochriw mountain. Colonel Hoare was immediately awoken from his afternoon nap and he proceeded to the local Police Station to receive whatever information was available on the landing. The Sergeant-in-Charge however, had already bravely made his way, single-handed, up to the mountain with half of the weapons of the neighbourhood - one rifle! Colonel Hoare then set about commandeering all passing cars and arranged for six brewery lorries to block the roads on the High Street to Rhymney Bridge and at Penuel Row.

Everyone at large was stopped and their identity cards examined and LDV volunteers mustered at Albion Square in readiness, armed with large knives or any other lethal weapons that they could lay their hands on. Hoare then went to check his defences at Penuel Row and Rhymney Bridge and in an out-lying defence post at the Rhymney Water Works. Satisfied with their invincibility he then returned to his troops at Albion Square to await events. In the meantime a message had got through that the women of Pontlottyn had gone up to the Fochriw mountain armed with knives for a head-on assault. The Battle of Albion Square however, was destined never to reach the columns of the military archives when it was discovered that what had been seen as invading German parachutists were in fact, just five back-fires from one of our own passing aeroplanes!

These are the officers of 'A' Company who drilled, inspected, trained and supervised the activities of the local Home Guard unit and amongst the group are Teddy Gower, Pete Shepherd, Harry Breen, Jones 'Cloth Hall', Harold Burnell and Eddie Williams.

Allied to the Home Guard and working very closely with them was the Rhymney Decontamination and Rescue Party which was responsible for stepping in after an act of aggression, removing all impurities from the scene and safeguarding any victims. This was the Rhymney 'B' Squad detachment in 1941.

One of the Brewery's strengths was its staff welfare commitment and in particular, its consideration for its retired members and their widows and widowers. The above group consists of retired employees and their relatives and friends who are getting together for a social evening. The many well-known faces include Esther Meade, Marie Jones, Dwynwen Lyons, the author's mother Ceinwen Jones, Marie 'Garno', Amelia Williams, Dilys Davies, Vano Gwalia, Dai 'Dowlais', Rowland Tuck, 'Big Arthur' Jones, Bob Phillips, Dai White, Hilda Price, Glenys Pritchard, Gwyneth Williams, Trevor Davies, Betty Rees, Mrs Newell, Myfanwy Jones the organist, Penno Beynon, Dilys Tyrell, Mrs Smith, Sarah Davies, Brychan Williams, Steve Pritchard, Brewer, John Morgan, Gwen Harris, Marie 'Force' Morgan, Johnny 'Coker' Williams, Ivor Cooke and Jan Poleman.

Sporting activities were always on the priority list of the Brewery's agenda with all sections, up to the Chairman participating. Here is the 1947 Andrew Buchan's Cricket Club which consisted of, from top left - EE Jenkins, EJ Harris, JDG Taylor, HE Howells, JH Thomas, E Evans, WT Evans, I Davies and H Lloyd the Umpire. In the front row are DJ Davies, ET Jones, WG Cornes, Col. JD Griffiths, JR Jones team captain, Lt. Col. GL Hoare CBE, the Company Chairman, NWG Taylor DSC vice captain, DR Cox and RW Jones.

Another happy party at the Brewery's New Year's Eve Dance in 1952 which consisted of, from the left - the author Marion Evans (née Jones), her father Tommy 'Aberystwyth' Jones who worked as a drayman with the Brewery from 1950 to 1967. Rene Matthews (now Jones), Evan 'Uncle Dai the Shop' Jones, Betty Jones, David Davies and Eddie Jones.

A cup-winning pool team display their trophy at Rhymney's Brewery Club. To be seen are Keith Knox, Dennis Roberts, Sam and wife Jane, past landlords of the Farmers Arms, Glyn Owen, Dai (Reb) Jones, Dai (The Ras), Dai (The Post) Williams and Graham Gilbert.

This is the retirement party of Gladys Bailey who worked in the bottle-cleaning department in the 1950s. In the back row are Mona Davies, Blodwen Price, May Francis, Peno Beynon, Esther Doyle, Doreen Jones, Glenys Pritchard, Marie Morgan, Rita Brooks, Marie Garno, Dilys Davies and Dwynwen Lyons. In front are Annie Lewis, Rene Jones (Matthews), Mrs Anthony, Lena Lester, Helena James, Gladys Bailey, Olwen Jones, Mona Williams, Betty Rees, Hilda Price, Gwyneth Williams and Anne Lewis.

This is the inaugural committee of the Brewery's first Sports Club which was initiated in the late 1950s. Their new clubhouse was opened at the south end of Clarendon Row and later became a Boys Club and then a builder's store. From top left, the committee consisted of Davies 'The Chemist', Glyn 'The Baron' Thomas, Bill Pulman, David Morgan, John 'Coker' Williams, unknown, John Newell and unknown. At the bottom of the picture are Jackie Woods, John Davies, Ron Cox, Eirwen Morgan, John Henry Thomas and Ken Newell.

The most important members of the organisation were the canteen staff who ran their premises in the now Brewery Club. Waiting to get back to the hot stove are Cassie Blewett, Doreen Sullivan, Megan Hulbert, Manageress Mrs Batten, Pat Davies, Blod Edwards and Sarah Davies.

The much-heralded 'Gang of Nine', all ex employees of the Brewery who were responsible for the re-birth of Rhymney's landmark known as 'The Bent Iron'. In the picture are, left to right - Len Ward, Jack Smith, David Jones steward of the Brewery Club, Ron Magness, David Moberley, Tom Davies, John Griffiths, Gwyn Jenkins and Clive Breen.

The original 'Bent Iron' was erected on the Fochriw mountain overlooking Rhymney in 1935 as a base to stabilise huge bonfires. Around the tall girder, which was embedded firmly in the earth, were built layer upon layer of railway sleepers which, when set alight could be seen for miles around. Bonfires have been constructed for centuries all over the country to commemorate passing events such as in 1918, to celebrate the end of World War One. In 1887 The Queen Victoria Jubilee generated 3,000 beacons nationwide and of course, 400 years later, we still mark the nation's deliverance from Guy Fawkes' gunpowder plot each year on November 5th. Our 1935 'Bent Iron' had, by 1979, vanished through weathering and open-cast coal mining which was when the innovative 'Gang of Nine' took it upon themselves to reconstruct the now lost landmark.

Their first task was to secure a 40 foot length of girder which they acquired from the ruins of the then demolished Rhymney Brewery and to patiently bend it into the arched shape of its predecessor. Their second task was to transport it manually across the mountain from Fochriw to its venue overlooking Rhymney, fuelled by the odd 'wee dram' on the way. As they battled on, their lusty chanting of the 'Hi Ho, Hi Ho song from *Snow White and The Seven Dwarfs'* could be heard resonating across the valley. On arrival the rail was firmly embedded in the ground in readiness for the next commemorative bonfire and everyone shook hands on a job well done. The original plan was to christen their achievement with a whole bottle of whisky but the members of the intrepid party were so wet and cold on that February morning, that just a minimum amount was poured on their edifice and the remainder used for internal thermal insulation!

The 1979 'Bent Iron' has since been rebuilt yet again in 2005 thanks to the efforts of David Jones, his wife Lena, Zoe Williams and Debbie Powell who were the driving force behind a new scheme for a more permanent structure to be erected This was to involve the support of the Rhymney Communities First Partnership Board, The Gwent Association Voluntary Organisations (GAVO), The Community Planning Key Fund and Groundwork Caerphilly. From the funding provided and through artist/designer Godfrey Phillips, was born the new 'Bent Iron' to be erected on the spot of the original landmark.

Of the original 'Gang of Nine' the above four, all ex Brewery employees, attended to witness the official opening of the re-born 'Bent Iron' in 2005, which was blessed by local vicar Marilyn Adsetts. They were Gwyn Jenkins, Len Ward, David Jones of the Brewery Club and David Moberley.

During the hot dry summer of 1976 a group of firefighters was formed at the Rhymney Brewery (by then Whitbread Wales), to help the over-taxed local Fire Service through the drought period. A Whitbread van was converted to serve as a fire engine and was furnished with the full range of hoses, extinguishers, jacks, breathing apparatus and resuscitation equipment. They were to again re-group in November 1977 because of the firemen's strike. Led by Ron Moseley, himself a part-time fireman, the team included Paul White also a part-time fireman, Alan Viney an ex full-time fireman, David Morgan, Ron Magness, Freddie Lewis and Glyn Morris all of whom are seen in this photograph.

ESTABLISHED 1839

ALL COMMUNICATIONS TO BE ADDRESSED TO THE COMPANY

ANDREW BUCHAN'S BREWERIES, LIMITED

BREWERS, WINE & SPIRIT & CYDER MERCHANTS

DIRECTORS:
COL. J. D. GRIFFITHS. D.L. J.P. CHAIRMAN.
P. W. KEMP-WELCH. O.B.E.
N. W. G. TAYLOR. D.S.C.
J. E. MARTINEAU.
D. R. Cox.
J. D. G. TAYLOR.
M. F. JUPP.
MASON H. SCOTT.

BREWERIES OFFICES
RHYMNEY
MON.

TELEGRAMS
BUCHAN'S RHYMNEY

TELEPHONE
RHYMNEY 212

OUR REFERENCE
DRC/NB.

YOUR REFERENCE

DATE
17th. July, 1956.

This is a letterhead of Andrew Buchan's Breweries Ltd. in July 1956 when the Board of Directors consisted of Col. JD Griffiths the Chairman, PW Kemp-Welch, OBE, NWG Taylor,DSC, JE Martineau, DR Cox, JGD Taylor, MF Jupp and Mason Scott.

The Brewery Club was constructed from the old Rhymney Drill Hall in 1974 for the benefit of its employees and their families and has seen a wide range of activities take place within its four walls. Members are gathered here in 1978 for a party to mark the sad occasion of the closure of the Brewery. Among the crowd are Bill 'Brychan' Williams, Ken Morgan, David Jones manager of the Club, Abe Morgan, Edgerton White, John O'Brien, Sid Jones, Elfryn Williams, Trevor Davies, Len Berry, John Meyrick, Clive Breen, Glyn Pritchard, John Meredith, Evan Davies, Glethyn Moon, Dai White (senior and junior), Geoffrey Jones, Jeffrey James, Sid Moberley, Mike Evans, Dai Price, Jimmy 'Brychan' Williams, Gareth Williams, Lyn Jenkins, Geoffrey Dallimore, Cyril Phillips, Malcolm Shute, Islwyn John, Godfrey Lewis, Peter Jenkins, Gwyn Jenkins, Jack Smith, Alan Jones, Des Leadington, Thomas Henry Davies, Frankie Minton, Danny O'Brien, Ron Jones, Ron Magness, Glyn Burrows, Ken James, Glyn Morris, David Davies, John Moore, Neville Root, Alan Betts, Tom Davies and Alan 'Chunky' Elliot.

The Queen's Golden Jubilee in 2002 was celebrated in fine style with a party in the Farmers Arms. Enjoying themselves are, at the back, Carol Walters, Susan Meredith landlady and Yvonne Pinch. In front are Joan Moseley, Verena Harris, Lena Jones and Janice Jenkins.

The Brewery Club around 1982 collected the grand total of £1200 for a local charity for the blind. Displaying their awards are to be seen a charity member, David Jones, Club Steward, Bill Proudly representative of the Blind Association, Lena Jones, another charity organiser, Barbara Hulbert and Tony Hulbert.

This special night out in Cardiff for ladies of the Brewery included the above group who, from left to right are Connie Jones, Gwyneth Williams, Alice Meredith, May Francis, Margaret Jones, Freda Smith, Winnie Horrigan (Jones), Olive Jones, Glenys Davies, Hilda Price, Lena Lester, Rene Jones (Matthews) and Megan Davies.

1939 was Andrew Buchan's Centenary Year and it was celebrated in admirable fashion in June of that year, with a cross-channel boat trip from Cardiff to Weston-Super-Mare. Joining the Rhymney contingent for the day were workers from Crosswell's Brewery, Cardiff and the excursion was well publicised in a two-page article in the Western Mail. In the front of the group, left to right are Managing Director JD Griffiths, Chairman Col. GL Hoare, Co. Secretary WJ (Bill) Jones and General Manager William Jones. Behind can be made out Tommy Sims and Cyril Pearce (both of whom were later killed in the war), Frank Morgan, Jack Jones, Tom Price, Ernie Humphries, John Rees Jones, Doug Humphries, Dewi Protheroe, Albert Marshall, William Lloyd, Horace Evans, Jack English, George Turner, Will Jenkins (Blacksmith), Jim Trunks, Willie Dallimore, Evan Jenkins, Harry Ogbourne, Howard Evans, Guyn Davies, Ron Cox, Dai Small, Bob Price, Granville Cornes, Ron Morgan, George Ogbourne, Reg Edwards, Jim Bucknell, Harry Lloyd, Len Berry, Glyn Richards, P McDermot, Bert Ash, Walter Williams, Cerris Moseley, Tommy Smith, Ernie Dibben, Pat Kennedy, Fred Berry, Tommy Harris, John Davies, Alma Durham, Olwen Baynham, Marie Summers (Jones), Myfanwy Jones, Annie Howells, Mary Price, Dai Glencross, Betty Rees, Duynwen Lyons, Marie Davies, Nina Smith, Annie Jenkins, Elizabeth Crowley, Ivy Rawle, Rene Matthews (Jones), Marie Hughes, Cynthia Minton, Hetty Burton, Megan Lloyd, Rene Webber, Phyllis Harris, Louise Clease and Reg Edwards.

This is the 1952 cricket team of the Andrew Buchan's Sports Club preparing for action. From top left are: T Kedward, D Protheroe, EJ Harris, Ron Harris and D Rees. Middle are: JH Thomas, A Prosser, HE Howells, and T Sulvan. Front are: DI Davies vice Captain, WG Cornes, DR Cox, JR Jones Captain, Col. J Griffiths, NW Taylor and JDG Taylor.

A Christmas celebration night out for the ladies of the Brewery in 1965. From the left, clearly having a great time at the Plymouth Arms, Pentrebach, Merthyr Tydfil are Dwynwen Lyons, Rene Matthews (Jones), Glenys Pritchard, Doreen Price, Hilda Price, Olwen Jones, Margaret Jones, Gwyneth Williams, Esther (Doyle) Jones, and Verena Harris.

Bottling Shop Manager Abe Morgan seen here with his wife Winnie, receives a warm goodbye from his colleagues at his retirement party in 1982. Joining him in the photograph are Trevor Wall, Billy Phillips, Robin Badham, Terry Grande, Mike White, Philip Betts, Ron Magness, Mervyn Jones and Brian Edwards.

Another retirement celebration, this time for Gladys Bailey who is surrounded by her friends and colleagues Marie (Garno) Davies, Marie Morgan, Doreen Price, Glenys Pritchard, Hilda Price, Ann Lewis and Betty Rees.

Rhymney Brewery employees joined with those of Ely Brewery, Cardiff for a dinner in the capital not long after the merger of the two companies in 1959. The following names have been identified - Bill Jones, Terry Grande, Graham Lewis, Ivor Cooke, Bill Price, Peter Smith, Dai 'Dowlais', Brian Hodges, Jeffrey Dallimore, Ron Jones, John Henry Thomas, Tommy Edwards, Lena Williams, Denzil Williams, May Francis and Dilys Tyrell.

The Brewery's children's Christmas Party was an event very much looked forward to on the calendar. Held in the Brewery Club, David Morgan makes a fitting substitute for Santa Claus.

Another boat trip across the Bristol Channel for Brewery employees, but much earlier than the last, and this time to Minehead. No names supplied I am afraid.

There were lots of smiling faces at the Brewery's annual dinner held at The Castle Hotel, Tredegar in 1954. Enjoying themselves are, from top left - Eirwen Williams, Blodwen Jones, Dorothy Moberley, Margaret Jones, Rosalind Dwyer, Enid Jones and Joan White.

Betty Rees retired from the Brewery in 1974 and her friends gathered to present her with a canteen of cutlery. Betty was well known for her beautiful alto singing voice and she was in great demand to participate in concerts and other events. With her at her retirement party are Neville Root (Distribution Manager), Gwyneth Williams, Hilda Price, Steve Williams and Sid Brook.

Employees of the Rhymney Brewery set off at the start of their sponsored walk in 1969 to raise money for the mentally handicapped children of Monmouthshire. Among the participants, who raised £180 were Dilys Tyrell, Gareth Jones, Ken Birch, Gethin Morris, Peter Jenkins, Glethyn Moon, Islwyn John, Malcolm Shute, Billy Jones, Mair Jones, Ron Jones and Gwyn Jenkins.

When Rhymney's Drill Hall was converted into the new Brewery Club in 1974 i[t] brought all the additional room, facilities and provisions to enhance the socia[l] activities that could take place there. Here we see its steward David Jones and wif[e] Lena being presented with a 'wish you well' token by Ann of the Ladies' Darts Team. Standing behind are Jacqueline Griffiths, Nelly Tovcoscvy, Annette Morgan, Bett[y] Newell and Nancy Ward.

Another friendly get-together for the widows and retired ladies of the Brewery, th[is] time in 1980 with each having been presented with a bouquet of flowers. Among th[e] happy smiling faces are Dwynwen Lyons, Ceinwen Jones, Dilys Tyrell, Mar[ie] (Force) Morgan, Betty Rees, Esther Meade, Dolly Price, Penelope (Peno) Baynha[m] Margaret (Garno), Nancy Clogeigh, Mrs Newell, Gladys Bailey, Marie Morga[n] Vano Sibley, Dorothy (Dolly) Thomas, Annie Howells and Louise Clease.

Some employees of the Brewery enjoy a drink and concert at the Railway Club which was once situated next to Rhymney Station. Among them are to be seen Bill Goodwin, Tommy 'Aberystwyth' Jones, Elvet Jones, 'Nobby' Withers, Jackie Collins, Mr Wilson and Dai Evans.

The Transport Department of the Brewery get together in the Farmers Arms for a social event. Included in the photograph are Roy Evans, Bryn Thomas, Bill Jones, Dai Small, the Transport Manager and Clive Breen.

Female employees from various departments get together for a Christmas dinner in 1960 in the old Company Shop Storeroom, where they were allowed to make use of the facilities and cook themselves a festive meal. Enjoying their creations are Doris Williams (Birch), Gladys Bailey, Ann Lewis, Hilda Price, Glenys Pritchard, Freda Smith, Betty Rees, Winnie Jones, Margaret Matthews (Jones), Olwen Jones, Louise Clease and Betty White.

One noteworthy event in 1936 associated with the Brewery was the visit of King Edward VIII to the Lawn Company Shop on Thursday, November 19th where the unemployed were engaged in a number of projects. The miners sang to him 'Aderyn Pur' and 'Cwm Rhondda'. This visit marked his last public appearance before tha final radio broadcast, which, in less than a month, announced his abdication. Here he dismounts from the train at Rhymney Station where it is said, Mrs Wallis Simpson awaited him. The King was conducted around the Company Shop by Dr Tom Jones who recorded the event in the local newspaper. Edward VIII was extremely popular in South Wales where he was welcomed with wild enthusiasm and in the Company Shop, he chatted, laughed and joked freely with the groups of unemployed that he met.

Managing Director Mr MF Jupp retired in 1968 and was presented with a French-style carriage clock by his colleagues in this informal get-together. With him can be seen, from the left, Pat Lewis, Mair Jones, his secretary Muriel Pritchard, Dilys Tyrell and Myfanwy Jones.

The cellar workers of the Brewery display their awards at a darts competition that they organised annually as part of the Christmas festivities. From the left are: Alan Williams, Clive Jones, Neville Root, Bill 'Rocky' Jones, Kevin Harris, Dai 'The Gas' whose job included filling up gas cylinders, Ron Mumford, Sid McArthur and Ken Walters.

Betty Rees' retirement party attracted a host of well-wishers, some of whom are seen above. The men, from left to right are Idris Davies, Alan 'Chunky' James, Sid 'Sparrow' Stephens, Jeff Moberley, Les Pugh, Mike Evans, Paul White, Cliff Evans, Gwyn Jenkins, Dai 'Boom Boom' Davies who played a drum in the Rhymney Town Band, WC Jones and Abe Morgan. The ladies are Hilda Price, Betty Rees, Margaret Jones and Annie Moseley.

A rip-roaring sing-along of Brewery employees at the retirement party of Penelope 'Peno' Baynham at the Castle Hotel in Tredegar. Clearly having a great time of it are John Meredith (now manager of the Farmers Arms), Tudor Davies on the 'ivories', Glyn 'The Baron' Thomas, Brian Hodges and Glyn Morris.

*Retired employees of the Rhymney Brewery, then Whitbread Wales, gather outside
the bottling shop in the early 1970s before setting off on their Pensioners' Outing.
Most names have been found, thanks to the memory of ex Brewery employee John
Meredith who is now the proprietor of the Farmers Arms in Rhymney. From left to
right, front and back, can be seen David Morgan, Myfanwy Jones (Gwalia), Neville
Root, Gwyneth Williams, Matron Woods, Dwynwen Lyons, Glenys Davies, Sid
McCarthy, Dai (Boom Boom) Davies, Mrs Lewis, Betty Rees, Mr Smith, WC (Rocky)
Jones, Islwyn Edwards, Ernie Hodges, Hilda Price, Bill Dallimore, Johnny (Coker)
Williams, Dai Richards, Bill (Brychan) Williams, Trevor Davies, Dai (The Stores),
Howell Howells, Evan Jenkins, John Rees Jones, Len Berry, Bob Phillips, Jack
English, Fred Rees, Dai Harris (Dowlais), Len Ward and Thomas Henry Davies.*

*Another Brewery social evening, this time at the Brewery Club. From top left are
Terry Grande, Eric Morris, Abe Morgan, Neville Root, John Rees Jones, David
Morgan and Tom Henry Davies. In front are Dilys Tyrell, Ann Pritchard, unknown
and Verena Harris.*

Mrs Batten, the canteen manager's retirement party, photographed here with some of the many who attended. Roughly from the left are Les Pugh, Mike Evans, Paul White, Dai Thomas, Sid 'Sparrow' Stephens, Jeff Dallimore, Dai Moon, Cliff Evans, WC Jones, Mrs Batten and Idris Davies.

This small group in the Sampling Room included Dai Small the Transport Manager, Glyn Davies, Free-Trade Manager and Jack English-Cellar Service Manager.

New Year's Eve at the Brewery Club can always be relied upon to do justice to the festive season. Here, at the suitably garlanded entrance door can be seen some of the officers of the Club greeting their visitors. Seated is Edgerton White next to Keith Williams-Chairman, Garrett Morris-Treasurer and Ladies Committee member Collette Morris.

A formal occasion for Brewery members at the Brewery Club included the above group and from the left are Trevor Wall, Jeff Dallimore, Dai Morgan, Glyn Pritchard, Philip Betts, Ron Magness and Gwyn Jenkins.

Supervising the children's Christmas Party at the Brewery Club in the 1960s were Edgerton White, Thomas Henry Davies and Sid Prosser. Amid the happy smiling faces of the children can be seen Father (David Morgan) Christmas.

The Brewery Club Pool Team which in 2005, competed in the 4X Finals Championship in Coventry. At the back are Paul White, Chris Harris, David Jones (Club Steward), Keith Williams and Garret Morris (Club Treasurer). In front are Terry Meade, Colin Watkins and Matthew Williams.

The Brewery office girls take a deserved break during proceedings in 1940. At the back can be seen Joan Glencross, Pat Burton, Olga Blake and Myra Richards. Sat in the front are Ivy Rawle and Dwynwen Lyons.

Some canteen staff of the Brewery in the early 1970s were, from the left, Margaret Smith, Blod Edwards, Sarah Davies, Mrs Batten and Doreen Sullivan with husband Jim.

The End of Brewing in Rhymney

On 21st October 1977, Ken Mead the Managing Director of Whitbread Wales informed the workforce that the Rhymney Brewery would close the following year. Economic factors, the changing pattern of trade and the public swing from beer to lager had made the decision inevitable and it had, by then, been realistically anticipated by the workers. The final closure came on 27th April 1978. In the almost 140 years since Andrew Buchan had first run the Brewery, it had produced a staggering 7 million barrels of beer. All production was then transferred to Cardiff.

Before the Brewery was pulled down, its Andrew Buchan clock, which by now had been transferred from the gate-yard portal to the wall of the cooper's shop, was again removed and fixed to the east-facing wall of the Distribution Depot at the bottom o Surgery Hill. Here we see Ron Moseley, brothers John and David 'Doc' Jones and Windsor Walters undertaking the removal, watched by passer-by Elvet Dunn. The photograph was taken by ex Brewery employee Elvet Jones of Ras Bryn Oer Farm.

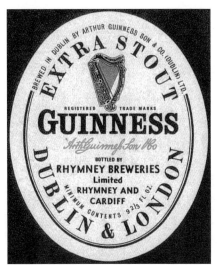

The Brewery closed in 1978 but their bottling and distribution centre remained in use until 1986, during which time the depot delivered t 1,000 outlets, later to be cut back to 600 when the Ipswich Road and Carmarthen depots took over some of their deliveries.

The new site of the Andrew Buchan clock in the bottling and distribution centre of the, then, Whitbread Wales concern. The building later housed the Whitbread Enterprise Centre.

After almost 140 years of brewing at Rhymney, the site is seen here being demolished and cleared after which it was to remain untouched for a number of years.

The boilerhouse chimney stands in grand isolation during the demolition period awaiting its fate. At one time run by John Morgan, the boilerhouse was situated next to the Brewers office and kept the Brewery supplied with the necessary heating that it required, particularly for such places as the mash-house. In the background can be seen Nantllesg, near to which were situated the Brewery's water tanks.

Again, in 1979, is to be seen a wider aspect of the Brewery in the stages of demolition, showing it in relation to the surrounding area. Alongside is Tir Edwards and immediately behind are Coronation Street and Queens Crescent. Several items of interest were removed and taken away to the Welsh Industrial and Maritime Museum at Cardiff Docks, including the plate 'Shoe Lane London 1839' shown earlier, together with a spiral staircase.

The site of the old Brewery as it now looks, with Tre Edwards to its right and where the supermarket Kwiksave was constructed, later to be replaced by Aldi in 2006.

Many relics remain throughout the town of the Buchan's brewing empire and one of considerable importance can be seen on an inside wall of the Brewery Club which proudly bears a large mural of the Rhymney Brewery, completed by Graham Gilbert in 1978. Gilbert was a senior lecturer at the Gwent College of Higher Education (BA Ions) and Head of the Student Support Service for the Faculty of Art and Design. On the right of the photograph is Mr ID Wilson, Managing Director of Whitbread, Wales unveiling the mural on 14th December 1978 accompanied by Mr Gilbert. The structure of the mural and its wood design was the responsibility of Ron Moseley who began working in the Brewery in 1949 as an apprentice carpenter and who remained there until its closure in 1978.

Mike Sullivan of Fochriw, an avid collector of memorabilia, worked for four years with the Rhymney Brewery in the mid 1970s in the brew house, cleaning the mash tins and milling the grain. His workmates were Ralph Smith and Mr Older, they working under the foremanship of Bill Dallimore. Here he proudly displays a treasured metal sign once used by Andrew Buchan's Breweries Ltd.

No longer standing, Brewery Row overlooked the Andrew Buchan Brewery until it was demolished in the mid 1960s. Built by The Rhymney Iron Company more than a century before, it accommodated workers in its local coalmines, ironworks brickworks and brewery.

An so it came to pass, the famous Hobby Horse stopped its roaming and is now only to be found, more often than not, as just a fading sign on a few old pubs here and there. Memories will remain however, of the huge impact that the Andrew Buchan Empire made on the town of Rhymney.

Epilogue

Thoughts remain divided on whether Rhymney Brewery could have survived to live another day had it not been taken over by Whitbread.

Rhymney had always been a valley-based company and a most successful one at that. This was ably demonstrated by a strong management and, just as importantly, a loyal workforce who together, enabled the Company to survive the many ups and downs in its fortunes brought about by economic and market forces during its long history.

Whitbreads, on the other hand, was a London-based company with a far greater national heritage, so what reason would they have to show such interest in Rhymney's invitation to take them over?

The takeover in itself was a controversial affair and attracted wide comments in the national press, with particular attention being paid to the fact that Whitbread's purchase of the Rhymney Company with its lands, buildings and licensed premises was completed in the year 1966, but, at its 1948 valuation! So, why **did** the resourceful Rhymney Breweries sell itself out? Possibly, or probably, because of the security that they considered the Whitbread 'umbrella' would provide them with, together with the immunity that might be gained from any undesirable acquisition from another source. Whatever the reasons, once the deal was done, it did not take long for it to be realised that over a period of time, Rhymney's once eminent status was gradually being undermined, causing feelings to run high in some quarters.

Whitbread products were introduced by Whitbread management, much to the detriment of Rhymney products and many popular and much-appreciated brands began to disappear. Varieties such as G.H.B. and B.B. draught beer, on which the brewery thrived, together with King's Ale, Ski Lager along with other well-known names were discontinued and fell by the wayside. Whitbread's acquisition of the Ely Brewery at Cardiff was seen by some as a further step towards centralizing their operations in the capital city, even though it was in the heart of their strongest competitors namely Brains and Hancocks. The eventual cessation of brewing at their most productive and profitable brewery at Rhymney added fuel to the theorists' view that this was part of a protracted plan, with Whitbread's mission accomplished! Who can now tell, whether the Hobby Horse would still be roaming the valley towns today had Rhymney Breweries not conceded to the wishes of the mighty Whitbread Empire?

Rhymney brewery calls 'time' after 140 years.

Acknowledgements

My sincere thanks go to the following people who have so willingly provided me with information, the loan of photographs, their memories and additional data for this project.

Nicholas Redman, Archivist with Whitbread plc, Chiswell Street, London; Malcolm Cox; David and Lena Jones, Rhymney Brewery Club; Garrett and Collette Morris; John and Susan Meredith, The Farmers Arms, Rhymney; Bill and Rene Jones; Elfryn and Anita Williams; Hilda Price; Muriel Pritchard; Mary Pulsford; Lyndon and Joan Vaughan; Mary Downey; Olga Pearson; Cynthia Jones (Minton); Iris Carey; The National Library of Wales; David Rhys Davies, verger St. David's Church, Rhymney; Abe Morgan; Edgerton White; Alan Roberts, photographer; Ralph Williams, Garden City; John Williams; Robert Lynch; Neil Protheroe; Norman Davies; Gwen Parfitt; Elvet Jones, The Ras; Mrs Moberley; Gwyn Davies; Mike Sullivan; Mr C. Burton; Prudence Allan; Jackie and Ken Jones; Robert Keddle; Mrs Joan Howells; Dai 'The Post' Williams; Lyndon Goode; Howard Evans; Peter Griffiths.

Bibliography

Rhymney Memories by Tom Jones
Echoes of Rhymney by EE Edwards
Whitbread in South Wales by Nick Redman
The Early History of the South Wales Ironworks by J Lloyd
Wilkins History of the Iron, Steel and Tinplate Trades by Charles Wilkins
A Look at Old Tredegar by Philip Prosser

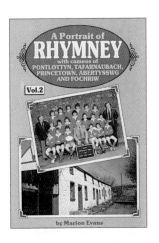
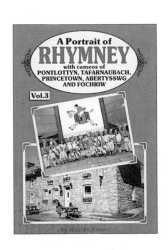
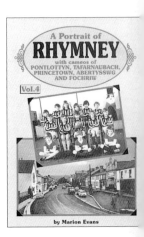

Additional available titles by author Marion Evans.